THE SIX FIGURE ATHLETE

CONVERT YOUR SKILLS INTO CASH

STORIES & STRATEGIES OF HIGH PERFORMERS

Self -n- DAYS
Publish 30
This Is The Year For
Your New Book

WWW.SELFPUBLISHN30DAYS.COM

Published by *Self Publish -N- 30 Days*

Printed in the United States of America

ISBN: 979-8-35365-428-5

1. Athletes 2. Sports 3. Leadership 4. Inspiration
The Six-Figure Athlete

Disclaimer/Warning:
This book is intended for lecture and informative purposes only. This publication
is designed to provide competent and reliable information regarding the subject
matter covered. The author or publisher are not engaged in rendering legal or
professional advice. Laws vary from state to state and if legal, financial, or other
expert assistance is needed, the services of a professional should be sought. The
author and publisher disclaim any liability that is incurred from the use or application of the contents of this book.

TABLE OF CONTENTS

>>

INTRODUCTION

Far too often in today's ultra-competitive world, the final numbers on the scoreboard judge the success of an athlete. Our wins and losses define us. The numbers we put on the stat sheet, the triumphant championships, and the blood, sweat, and tears we put into the game won't transfer to our bank account. At least, not right away.

Although our physical prowess took us far in life, we need more than just athletic gifts to become a six-figure athlete. If you play to win where winning counts, you can cash in on the lessons you'll learn from each of the authors in this book. As athletes, we've lived to constantly improve ourselves. Always striving for an unattainable level of perfection.

Developing the principles and skills for excelling in life will bring us long-term success even after our playing days come to an end. One of the ways we sought to gain a competitive edge during those days was by watching film. Not only did we watch our own film, but we also studied the greats. If you wanted to play like the best, you had to study the best.

With film, you can view it in real time, slow it down, and fast forward to see how things play out from different angles. If you're anything like me, you have plays that stood out to you more than others. It's the highlight tape from our glory days that plays in our minds, over and over again.

Game film allows us to see how we performed from a third-person perspective. When you watch yourself closely, you'll start to notice things you didn't notice before. You'll see some of the weird things you do. Some of the amazing things you do. You'll see where there's room for improvement. Being able to identify our strengths and weaknesses from afar helps define our priorities in practice. This gives us an opportunity to improve.

If you're like any of the authors in this book, I'm sure you'll focus more on the areas that need improvement than on the things you're already great at. After all, the goal is to improve and challenge yourself to get better, right? That's what this book is about. It's about performance—during and *after* your days as an athlete.

Use this book as your game film for the next season of your life. Use each of the skills and lessons these former athletes did well and find ways to implement them. Be sure to take heed of the areas they struggled with and make the necessary adjustments so you can have a different outcome.

Work through the good, the bad, and the ugly that comes with carving out a new lane for yourself post-sport. Enter this new chapter of your life with strength and guiding wisdom. Learn the strategies shared in each chapter so, you too, can convert your skills into cash.

CHAPTER ONE

OUT OF BOUNDS

By Kendra Brim

W hat happens when the lights go dim and the last whistle blows? What happens when you step out-of-bounds for the first time without limits or conventional boundaries? When a team sends the ball out-of-bounds during a basketball game, they lose possession. In the game of life, I was determined to never lose possession. The first time I stepped out-of-bounds was in 2011. I was scared and unsure of what would happen next in my life. Nonetheless, I knew whatever laid before me, I was going to win.

As a former Division I basketball athlete and receiving nineteen scholarship offers to play basketball, I was awarded a four-year basketball scholarship at Colgate University from 2007 to 2011. But it all started when I was eight years old during one of my visits to the local community center in Buffalo, New York.

On a fall afternoon in 1998, I begged my dad to let me play basketball with the boys who played in an after-school program at my local community center.

While sitting on the bleachers in an empty gym, I looked into my dad's eyes with tears and said, "I want to play basketball."

In reality, the tears came from me getting in trouble because I snuck into the gym instead of being in art class. But, surprisingly, my dad wasn't mad.

"Well, I don't know," he responded. "Basketball is more mental than physical, and I don't know if you are ready for it." I took that as a challenge. My loud "yes", coupled with my stern look glaring back in my dad's eyes, became the best decision I ever made. And, of course, my dad was right. Little did he know, he was preparing me for the game called life.

Throughout the years, I spent countless hours in the gym. Early mornings perfecting my shot. I travelled to various basketball camps across the country. Attended showcases featuring player-to-player matchups and days-long formats, often with consecutive games.

I would be remised if I did not thank my mom for driving and flying me literally everywhere across the country to tournaments and showcases. I always say she received a D1 Basketball Scholarship as well!

My biggest motivation came in the Summer of 2002. A parent in one of my Amateur Athletic Union (AAU) teams told me, "You will never play D1, D2, or D3 basketball. So, stop wasting your time and my daughter's time."

I constantly turned the ball over to the other team because of my goofy demeanor. My lanky stature caused me to fall face-first because I was not strong enough to battle older girls. The AAU team

I played for always played with older girls. Even though I was thir-teen and almost six feet tall, my stature did not equate to the percep-tion I was big and strong enough to handle the competition.

I knew I needed to prove this parent wrong because I did not want her sentiments to dictate my life. Moreover, proving her wrong sparked the inner compet-itiveness required for the game of basketball. I remember reading, "If you prove someone wrong without class, it doesn't really mean much. But, if you prove someone wrong with character, then your story can inspire mil-lions." This quote was the ultimate motiva-tion I needed to succeed. And that is exactly what I did.

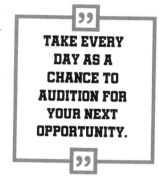

TAKE EVERY DAY AS A CHANCE TO AUDITION FOR YOUR NEXT OPPORTUNITY.

I have sought to perfect my game ever since then. I also remem-ber thinking to myself when I was a teenager, *I cannot wait to write about how I proved this parent wrong in a book.* It's crazy how life works. Thank you, *Six-Figure Athlete.*

I could write about time management, teamwork, and discipline, but if you are reading this book, you have heard that narrative before. However, someone rarely speaks about auditioning in the game of life. My mother always told me to show up and show out! You never know who is watching.

You will have bad days in life, but do not let that affect how you show up consistently. How many times have we seen players' future lives be affected due to their attitudes on the court? How often have we heard players say that was not a true reflection of them argu-ing with the referee or storming off the court? Take every day as a chance to audition for your next opportunity. It does not matter if you continue your athletic career or not.

Before I was a basketball player, I was a dancer and piano player. I even attempted to be the next Alicia Keys by picking up singing. Unfortunately, the singing part lasted only six months.

For each childhood activity I participated in, I auditioned in some way to be on the stage. Basketball was no different. I auditioned for each AAU team I played for. My high school varsity basketball team. Even for all nineteen schools until I received a scholarship to play basketball.

Once the lights dimmed in the Spring of 2011 and I stepped out-of-bounds, I continued to audition for several opportunities. After undergraduate school, with several small jobs in between, I auditioned for one of the greatest opportunities of my life: acceptance to the State University at Buffalo (UB), Jacobs School of Management, for my Master's in Business Administration.

> ONCE YOU KNOW WHAT FAILURE FEELS LIKE, DETERMINATION CHASES SUCCESS.
> KOBE BRYANT

While playing basketball as an undergrad, my GPA skimmed the requirements for graduate school acceptance. My GMAT math scores were not the best. After being denied from several graduate schools in 2011, I was told by one school never to apply again.

This narrative was eerily reflective of when I was twelve and was told that I would not play NCAA basketball. I did not accept that as my end of the audition. I still showed up to Act I.

ACT I

In 2011, I was denied acceptance to several graduate schools. I was told my GPA and GMAT were not high enough to be accepted. But, of course, I would not take "no" as an answer. I knew I wanted to go to graduate school, but I was not sure how that would happen just yet. I was not averse to hard work.

As former athletes, we know our destination, and we will work hard to get there. Immediately after undergrad, I worked as an AmeriCorps member, a Medicare Sales Agent for an insurance company, and freshman basketball coach at my high school alma mater. I enrolled in several local leadership programs and networked with many local organizations and not-for-profits. I figured if I gained work experience, I would be able to compile a resume where I could not be denied again.

ACT II

It was the summer of 2014. I heard about an invite-only open house for the University at Buffalo (UB) School of Management Master in Business Administration Program. I did not receive an invite in my email like many attendees, but I showed up anyway.

As athletes, we will show up because we never want to miss an opportunity. Based on the past, I knew I would have to show the dean of the school something different because I had previously been denied by so many schools.

When I arrived at the open house, I hesitated. The room I'd walked into seemed so big. Those same feelings I'd had as an early teenager playing basketball—reluctance and shyness came over me. Every question popped into my head. *Am I good enough? Will they accept me? Am I supposed to be in the room? Why would I have self-doubt now?*

I overcame someone telling me I would never play college ball. I refused to back down now.

The open house began with an introduction from the dean of students, followed by a presentation from current students and alumni.

During the presentation, I devised a plan to speak to the dean of students. I knew I would have to tell her a story—"The Life of Kendra Brim."

During one of my first jobs, I had a boss who was my advocate and ally. He would periodically call me into his office and ask me, "Why are you here?" I never fully understood his question. After the fourth or fifth time, he finally explained his question. He saw potential in me. He knew my life did not consist of a job sitting behind a desk all day. He told me I was so much more than my résumé. He would end our conversation by saying, "Own your story. Tell your story. No one can take that away from you."

> **I OVERCAME SOMEONE TELLING ME I WOULD NEVER PLAY COLLEGE BALL. I REFUSED TO BACK DOWN NOW.**

I took his advice. Taking a deep breath after the presentation, I walked up to the dean of students.

"Hi, my name is Kendra Brim," I said, with unshaken confidence. "You won't regret having me in your program."

She glared into my eyes and inquired, "Tell me why."

I proceeded to tell her about my resilience, leadership qualities, and determination. I weaved these qualities into my experiences. I spoke about the time I spent four months in Perth, Australia, living among the Aborigines.

I spoke about how the world is bigger than our backyard. Emphasized the importance of learning about new cultures. About appreciating differences and gaining a better understanding of the world around us.

These are all things modern businesses look for when hiring, and these traits are important in our world today.

The dean took a step back and said, "We want you in our school. Send your paperwork, and we will go from there."

I arrived at the event feeling shy and almost defeated and left feeling confident. The same moves would not win the game against the opponent the second time. Shortly after the open house, I received my acceptance letter under conditional circumstances. I had to maintain a 3.0 average and take a math class at a local community college before school started.

Of course, I showed up and showed out! I enrolled as a student in the UB MBA program the following semester.

ACT III

Spring of 2019, I graduated from the UB School of Management. It may be ironic I combined sports and acting in my story. As my dad always said, "Playing basketball is like a show. You audition, dance, perform, and the curtains are drawn at the end."

Whether you are looking to work for a company or thriving to become an entrepreneur, you are always auditioning. It never stops! You are not auditioning just in front of the casting director. You audition in front of the executive director, assistant director, choreographer, and set designer.

The National Collegiate Athletic Association (NCAA) released their 2020 Probability of Competing Beyond High School Figures and Methodology Report. This was based on the high school figures from the *2018-19 High School Athletics Participation Survey* and college numbers from the *NCAA's 2018-19 Sports Sponsorship and Participation Rates Report*.

According to the data, 540,769 boys participated in high school basketball, with 3.5% becoming NCAA participants and 1% being Division I athletes.

In addition, 399,067 girls participated in high school basketball, with 4.1% becoming NCAA participants and 1.3% Division I athletes. For both NBA and WNBA, approximately 1% of NCAA players get drafted annually. Thus, most college athletes have no choice but to audition every day for their next major role after college. These roles only exist out-of-bounds.

After years of auditioning, networking, and telling my own story, I gained creditability. I started my own diversity and inclusion consulting company, K. Savannah Consulting LLC. We are a firm focused on implementing strategies to maximize an organization's potential and shift the culture. This is my proudest accomplishment.

I used all my life experiences—playing basketball and traveling abroad—to create a company that would help improve the lives of everyone through a culture of inclusivity.

My greatest advice for anyone is to hone in on several soft skills learned during your athletic career. Those things can be self-confidence, flexibility, and assuming calculated risk.

Always remember to move beyond fear.

My question to you is, what will you do when the lights go dim, and the last whistle blows? Are you going to continue to audition? Are you going to continue to move beyond your fear? You get to decide.

As a competitive athlete, you never forget how to compete and show up and show out. Use those skills to be the best version of yourself out-of-bounds; don't live within the confines and limitations that others may set forth for you.

ABOUT KENDRA

Kendra Brim is a diversity, equity, and inclusion (DEI) and racial equity practitioner. She brings over ten years of experience working in project management, health care, not-for-profit organizations, and education. Kendra is the CEO and principal consultant of K. Savannah Consulting, a DEI firm focused on implementing strategies to maximize an organization's potential and shift overall in culture.

With her background in project management, managing projects upward of $10 million, Kendra has been a critical driver to success within organizations. Kendra focuses on increasing and promoting cultural competency by creating substantive learning and transparent formal opportunities. She prioritizes relationship-building and ensures each process is tailored to each organization's brand, mission, values, and goals.

Kendra Brim is a native of Buffalo, NY. She received a four-year Division I Basketball Scholarship to Colgate University, where she majored in Political Science and minored in African American Studies. Kendra has her Masters in Business Administration from the University at Buffalo, Jacobs School of Management, and a Diversity & Inclusion Certificate from Cornell's ILR School.

She is currently the executive vice president for the National Urban League Young Professionals. Kendra also serves on multiple community boards located in the City of Buffalo and nationwide. In addition, Kendra is the co-host of The Black Gems Dive In Podcast—a podcast where she discusses inclusive cultures and everything diversity, equity, and inclusion. To date, her proudest achievement was establishing Buffalo's Black Restaurant Week under the Buffalo Urban League Young Professionals in 2018.

Kendra@ksavannahconsulting.com

CHAPTER TWO

ADVANTAGES OF ADAPT-ABILITY

By Janet Conner

E lite athletes often say the game "slows down" for them. This allows them to notice and react to things happening around them that other players and spectators may overlook. The reason for this "slowdown" is the accumulation of countless hours and experiences on the field.

In 2001, Derek Jeter made a famous play in the ALDS series against the Oakland Athletics. With a runner on first, the A's hit the ball down the right-field line. Assessing the speed of both runners and monitoring their location, Jeter positions himself behind the two cutoff options. When the throw comes in from the outfield and sails over the cutoff players, Jeter is perfectly positioned to either throw to third to make a play on the batter or flip the ball home, which he does, successfully getting the out and preventing a run from scoring.

The fundamentals of the game become second nature to muscle memory. This frees the brain to take in more information from the things happening around it. With repetition of a task, like fielding a ground ball or swinging a bat, neurons in the motor cortex, cerebellum, and basal ganglia are activated.

New neural pathways form between the central nervous system and the muscles involved in the task. This allows the task to be completed with minimal conscious effort. The great news is that this ability transcends sport-specific skills and easily transfers to the other important skills learned on the field, like situational leadership and adaptability.

As a Fortune 500 executive, I can easily identify skills I use in the workplace every day that are second nature to me. Not because of anything I learned in the classroom, but because I spent years developing those skills on the softball field. I've been a student of the game of baseball well before I even knew what that meant. Growing up, if the St. Louis Cardinals weren't on the TV, they were on the radio. Our summer vacations when I was a kid were to Omaha to watch the College World Series. In fourth grade, when my friends were dressing up as princesses and witches for Halloween, I went as my favorite player, Todd Zeile.

The fundamentals of softball came very naturally to me (thanks, Dad, for those genes). Of course, I still had to practice and refine those skills, but my brain was also free to begin learning the nuances of on-field leadership in my chosen position: shortstop. The shortstop is the de facto leader of the infield. You have a place to be in nearly every scenario, and you often make split decisions on where the ball should go.

In a gap hit to the outfield, you must be confident and loud. The outfielder chasing down the ball needs to hear you over the opposing team's cheers. More importantly, over all the parents in the stands making their own decisions on where the ball should be thrown. Otherwise, precious seconds are lost when the outfielder retrieves the ball and turns to the field, trying to figure out what to do with it.

Between pitches, you ensure everyone knows how many outs there are and where the play is. You communicate with your teammates about who is covering which base in various scenarios. You are the chief communication officer of the defense.

I loved being a shortstop. Decisive, quick-thinking, energetic, and vocal was (and still is) my natural habitat, and these are the qualities I have always associated with leadership.

As I progressed beyond the pitching machine, I decided to learn how to pitch. I wasn't as naturally gifted in this position as other pitchers I encountered, but for many of the teams I was on, I was at least good enough that I was often splitting time between pitching and playing shortstop. I had an incredible pitching coach who taught me not just how to be a good pitcher physically but also mentally.

If you've ever known a great pitcher, you may notice some common mental traits they exhibit on the field. In the most stressful situations, with the game on the line, they know how to stay calm—stoic even. Their emotions never get too high or too low.

In my early days of pitching, this was entirely foreign to me. I was constantly in shortstop mode between pitches, announcing where the plays were and directing traffic on the infield.

A pitcher's brain is constantly at work. They need to know the ideal strategy for each hitter on the opposing team. Every pitch provides real-time feedback to be analyzed, and the data is immediately applied to the next pitch. You miss your target because your release point was slightly off, or maybe you didn't have the right amount of hip rotation.

Some pitchers may appear to come off as slightly arrogant. This, again, is a necessity of their position. The moment an ounce of self-doubt enters a pitcher's mind, they lose the advantage over the batter. They must also have an impossibly short memory to immediately regain that confidence after a walk, wild pitch, or home run.

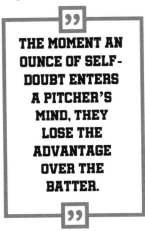

THE MOMENT AN OUNCE OF SELF-DOUBT ENTERS A PITCHER'S MIND, THEY LOSE THE ADVANTAGE OVER THE BATTER.

There's no question the pitcher is always in a leadership role. They set the pace and tone of the entire game. A play cannot start until they make it happen. They know when to slow things down and when to speed up their attack. Given the immense mental load the pitcher must process, their leadership is more often demonstrated in their actions and demeanor than with their voice.

The more I learned about the mental and emotional skills I needed to be a successful pitcher, the more my assumptions about leadership and, more specifically, *my* leadership style began to evolve. I found my brain capacity quickly maxed out by the focus I needed to have on my technique and the mental battle with each hitter. I learned that the infield didn't need more than one decision-maker and that the best way to lead as a pitcher was to be quiet. To focus on the tone and pace I was setting through my actions.

Both positions, shortstop and pitcher, are leaders on the field. In learning to play them both successfully, I learned an important lesson about leadership. I learned not only that there are different *styles* of leadership but also that any person can exhibit more than one style based on the situation they are in and the attributes of others around them. What I know now as a professional is that this is a valuable, transferrable skill called "adaptability" that many athletes have ingrained in them.

The idea behind the concept of adaptability is we all have a natural "comfort zone" or default leadership style, which will naturally come about without much thought or intentionality on our part. For me, that is more of a decisive style. As long as I'm in a position where I am, in fact, the expert or the most knowledgeable person in a given situation, I tend to make a decision quickly and move on to the next task at hand.

Given this tendency, it should come as no surprise that after starting a career in health care IT, I found myself in a project management role. With a project team of nearly 100 individuals across various companies (vendor, client, third party), I always saw my responsibility as "chief communication officer" on the project.

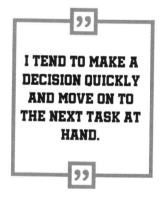

I TEND TO MAKE A DECISION QUICKLY AND MOVE ON TO THE NEXT TASK AT HAND.

With so many moving pieces, deliverables, and deadlines to hit, there simply wasn't time to gain consensus and analyze every little decision that had to be made. Higher levels of collaboration had to be reserved for the more impactful decisions. And in a project of this size, there are hundreds of little decisions that need to be made regularly.

A small team and I were flying to South Carolina for a physician training event that started at 7 am the following day. After making it to Atlanta, our connecting flight scheduled to depart at 6 pm got delayed several times. First to 8:30, then 10:00, then 11:00, and as

11:00 approached, we learned it would now be after 11:45 pm at least.

The team looked to me. Rental cars were going fast. Do we hope the 11:45 departure time sticks and risk rescheduling the entire event if the flight gets canceled? Or do we grab a car and drive the three and a half hours to ensure we got there in time to conduct the training?

> **I WAS THE SHORTSTOP. IT WAS MY CALL TO MAKE, AND TIME WAS TICKING.**

It felt like I was playing shortstop again, and the ball had been hit into the gap. Like an outfielder chasing down the ball, listening for me to tell them where to throw it, my team was looking at me to decide whether to wait out the plane or rent a car and drive. I had incomplete information. I had no more knowledge of the circumstances than the others on my team, but I was the project manager. I was the shortstop. It was my call to make, and time was ticking.

After weighing options with my team, I ultimately decided we would rent a car and drive. We kept each other awake, listening to '80s songs. By the time we checked into the hotel, we had ended up with only a couple of hours of sleep before having to be onsite. Even with opposition, the team did a flawless job, and the event was completed as planned.

I can't tell you how often there were last-minute travel issues that needed a quick and decisive resolution. Associates missed flights. Flights were delayed. Snowstorms required an impromptu change in schedule.

Once a team member forgot to book a rental car prior to her flight, and when she arrived, the airport was completely sold out of cars due to a big sporting event in the area that same day. I had already made the two-hour drive to my client's site, but I had to hop back in the car and drive to pick her up so she could be onsite to work with the client.

In the grand scheme of things, these quick little decisions were not terribly impactful to the overall project, so my default authoritative style worked great. There wasn't time to consult a lot of people. For someone who struggles to take the initiative or doesn't feel empowered or sure of themselves, this type of quick decision-making would be uncomfortable at a minimum and crippling at worst. But for a former shortstop, they are just part of another day on the job.

Even within the same role as a project manager, there were times I had to act much more like a pitcher, where it wasn't so much my decisive actions but my demeanor that influenced the project team. The go-live of a new software system can be a highly stressful time. Especially for people who are not highly tech-savvy, new software can mean they are no longer as confident in their abilities to complete their work. People manifest these emotions in various ways, from denial to anger to disengagement. As a project manager, I have been yelled at more times than I expected going into this job.

In those moments, it felt like I'm on the mound with the game on the line and the cleanup batter stepping into the box. I know I must master my emotions and lead by example. They say misery loves company, and I think stress and fear often do too.

If I let myself get flustered and show anything other than being calm and confident, the client will probably feel even more stressed. I'm a pretty good flyer, but sometimes there is a noise I hear or a bump I feel that is new and unsettling. I look immediately at the flight attendant. I've never seen one of them demonstrate anything other than calm. I think pitchers would make great flight attendants.

In sports, being a utility player can be a great asset in that it increases the number of scenarios in which you can help your team win. The workplace is no different. Being great at one thing, especially in certain fields, can be quite lucrative, but being effective in various scenarios often brings new opportunities. For a highly skilled leader, the secret sauce is not just in having multiple tools and styles in your arsenal, but also in knowing when to use each one.

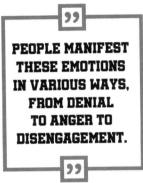

PEOPLE MANIFEST THESE EMOTIONS IN VARIOUS WAYS, FROM DENIAL TO ANGER TO DISENGAGEMENT.

It is important to adapt your behavior in various scenarios, but it's also useful to adapt your leadership style when it comes to interactions with various individuals. Whether you are leading a project or you are hierarchically a people manager, each person on your team will need or want something different from you, based on their knowledge level in the work they are doing.

As an athlete, you've undoubtedly experienced this. When I was a young T-ball player learning the game, I needed a lot of direction from my coach. I had to learn the rules of the game and the fundamental skills to play it, like hitting, fielding, and throwing.

Once I had the fundamentals down, I needed oversight as I started practicing the repetitions needed to form good habits and muscle memory. In my teenage years, I needed less direction on how to do things, but with so many activities and competing priorities in my world, my dad spent as much time convincing me to make time to put in the work as he did coaching me on things like technique. At the collegiate level, much of the individual conditioning work was delegated. I went to the weight room, the track, and the batting cage when my schedule allowed, often without the oversight of my coach.

If you think back on your own athletic experiences, you may recognize a similar pattern in how you engaged with your coaches at various stages of your development. With that context, it's easy to see how professionals in the workplace are like athletes. The support and direction they need from their managers may vary from person to person, and their needs may change over time as they gain proficiency in doing a given task.

I currently manage associates with various tenures in their positions. With those who are newer, I schedule more frequent one-on-one time with them to help them navigate the "how-to" of their job. I begin by having them shadow a senior member of the team doing the work. Then I have the senior team member shadow *them* doing the work before finally letting the newer associates work independently, asking questions, of course, when needed.

My leadership style has evolved over time. When I was new in a managerial role, I felt the need to do more educating and shadowing than was probably necessary. I felt accountable for my team's performance, so I felt more comfortable having my eyes on all their work.

Even the most talented athletes are always learning. Delegation has been a skill I have had to practice over time, and I still have to be thoughtful and intentional about it today. Fortunately, I have had great mentors and leaders help me learn the importance of delegation and coach me on how to do it correctly. By delegating the right work at the right time, I am empowering my team and giving them an opportunity to stretch themselves. To learn, and make mistakes

MY LEADERSHIP STYLE HAS EVOLVED OVER TIME.

in a safe space. In other words, I am helping them grow, and that is my favorite part of being a leader.

When an athlete dedicates years of their life to a sport and becomes a deeply-knowledgeable student of the game, they learn so much more than sport-specific skills like how to swing a bat, kick a ball, or shoot a three-pointer.

If you have learned to be adaptable in the field, you can easily transfer that skill to be adaptable in the office. Having leaders who can represent the company well in any situation, build strong relationships with clients, and can grow a team of people is something companies will and do pay top dollar for.

ABOUT JANET

Originally from Jefferson City, Missouri, Janet Conner is a health care IT consulting and operations executive. She holds a Master's Degree in Business Administration from the University of Kansas and a Bachelor's Degree in Applied Mathematics from the University of Missouri-Rolla (now known as Missouri S&T).

Janet was a two-sport collegiate athlete at MST, competing in both indoor track and softball. Janet held many school records on the softball field that still stand today. She was inducted into the MST Athletic Hall of Fame in 2014 as an individual and again in 2016 as part of the 2004 Women's Softball Team.

In the Kansas City community, Janet is actively involved with the Leukemia and Lymphoma Society, being named Kansas City's Woman of the Year in 2015 for her fundraising efforts and serving on the Board of Trustees from 2017 to 2019. She is a 2020 inductee into the MST Academy of Miner Athletics, and she is a 2022 recipient of the MST Distinguished Young Alumni Award. Currently, Janet lives in Kansas City with her husband, Aaron, and dog, Lana.

As an avid sports fan, she enjoys watching the St. Louis Cardinals and Kansas City Chiefs. She continues her love for athletic performance and coaching as a Group Fitness instructor with Genesis Health Clubs.

CHAPTER THREE

AN ATHLETE'S WEALTH STANDARD

By Kezia Conyers

Most people say sports create an environment that allows you to triumph, fail, learn new concepts, and engage with people from different as well as similar demographics and socioeconomic backgrounds. Enhancing one's communication skills, self-discipline, and interpersonal skills are all fundamental in sports.

The wealth standard is a mindset. I think about how, as a society we are so driven by money. Individuals often think status and a plush bank account are solely success. The true wealth standard is about having the fortitude to ascend in every aspect of life. It is about being effective in your business and career, operating at an optimal level due to a healthy lifestyle. Constantly working on physical and mental fitness is imperative to be the best version of *you* for yourself and your family.

Thinking back on my time as an athlete, I was never taught how the same skills I used in sports could not only help me improve my self-identity, but could also lead to abundance in every area of my life.

> **THE TRUE WEALTH STANDARD IS ABOUT HAVING THE FORTITUDE TO ASCEND IN EVERY ASPECT OF LIFE.**

In an athlete's career, during what is called "the grassroots stage", the foundation should be set for their success. This is the time when an athlete's mindset is cultivated and developed with pure intentions from coaches and mentors. If executed properly, the only motive is to enhance the athlete's skills and abilities to perform. They understand it's about the player's growth and having fun while playing sports. This approach will render mindsets in athletes applicable for the rest of their lives.

AREAS OF FOCUS

Habits, routines, and mindset are three areas of focus for operating at an optimal level. These things are used to develop athletes. Successful people are constantly seeking new ways to accomplish goals. They understand a paradigm shift must happen. The way we perceive things and understand and interpret situations is vital to a wealthy life.

The correlation between what athletes do and what wealthy people do daily is similar. Therefore, it is imperative for the people who engage closely with athletes to recognize their influence and how it assists in the development of those skills mentioned above.

In his book, *7 Habits of Highly Effective People,* by Stephen Covey, the first habit is about being proactive.[1] We are responsible for our own lives. We need to know the importance of taking the initiative. This is a notion I express to my team all the time. When it comes to academics or improving certain parts of the game, it is ultimately up to them to handle their business. I can put them in a position to thrive and advise them, but I can't do it for them.

Having upperclassmen who make sure teammates are on time to study hall, turn in their weekly class assignment sheet, and encourage teammates to get extra shots in between classes all contribute to our mission as a team. Coaches love players who take the lead on certain things within a program. A player-coached team is always better than a coach-coached team.

Taking the initiative helps you through your processes as an athlete to garner the tools you need. It also teaches how to become a self-starter. Initiative, or the impulse to take action, prompts people to continue to learn and seek ways to improve their craft. As a result, you gain confidence in yourself.

Initiative is a life skill that will be needed in adulthood. Wealthy and successful people challenge themselves.

ROUTINES

Routines develop a sense of discipline. Routines and daily habits go hand in hand. Both routines and daily habits teach us about ourselves, what to do and how to do things, and knowing how to manifest our visions through adjustments. This isn't just a one-method-fits-all deal. Every person must cultivate what works for them, then adjust when

---

1 Covey, Stephen. 7 Habits of Highly Successful People. Free Press, 1989.

needed. Practice daily habits that work for you. It may be at certain times in the morning every day, exercising, learning something new, journaling, meditating, listening to podcasts, or reading.

Wealthy and successful people know this is essential to life's order, but so does an athlete. College athletes are routine-oriented individuals. The schedules in college structure a day of responsibilities needing to be fulfilled. This is setting a standard to implement throughout your life. I still adhere to practices I learned as an athlete. I wake up early (5:00 am), wrote out a schedule for the week, and then broke down my daily to-do list. I stay aligned with my daily goals by actively operating with purpose. It instills a high level of productivity when I am able to see what needs to be accomplished each day.

I STAY ALIGNED WITH MY DAILY GOALS BY ACTIVELY OPERATING WITH PURPOSE.

EMOTIONAL INTELLIGENCE

The intangibles and experiences of athletes provide the tools needed to move forward. Emotional intelligence in athletes consists of how to assess their environment to improve in areas or adjust when needed. Their confidence builds up because of competing against others. The get-knocked-down-and-get-back-up mentality expands their mental fortitude. Athletes are goal-oriented, driven by completing tasks and accomplishing objectives.

During competition, there will be instances when players need to adapt. A team always goes into a game with a plan or strategy to implement, but things do not always go as planned. Injuries may occur, foul trouble may occur, we may not be making shots, etc. In the grand scheme of the season, unexpected situations will always arise.

A few years ago, our team was slated to win the conference championship. We were having a great season. Going into the final second half of our season, our leading scorer left the team due to personal reasons. Then our starting post player suffered a sprain (medial collateral ligament) in her knee. Two weeks later, our second leading scorer tore the anterior cruciate ligament in her knee.

During that season, those players learned to face adversity head-on and quickly adjust to the circumstances they were experiencing. It stretched them mentally. In those moments, my players learned how to stay composed while working together to devise a plan to finish our season successfully.

This is an example of how the sport applies to life. Along our journey in life, we will encounter situations where emotional intelligence is needed. Athletes can learn this skill early in life.

In 2022, athletes are now a brand. Conduct yourself as such. The dominance of social media has created multiple avenues to establish relationships and find mentors. Learn from those who are thriving in the industry you want to master after sports. Many people will have the same interests as you. Follow those individuals, research, and ask for advice.

Furthermore, understand that what you present on your social media page represents you. My position as a college coach is to relay this message to my athletes. So, my message to them has to extend beyond the basketball court. Financial gains are in place for athletes using their social media pages to their advantage.

One thing I love about social media is that it allows athletes to tell their own stories. Athletes can help other people through sharing and storytelling. The truth is athletes are so much more, but the notion must be presented to an athlete when they are playing. Coaches, like myself, must be receptive to learning more about the branding industry and how it functions pertaining to the athletes. We must convey a message to players that what you represent is who you are. The way you conduct yourself daily on and off campus is critical.

The National College Athletic Association has granted athletes the opportunity to benefit from their name, image, and likeness. Governors in certain states have signed the NIL bill into law.

ATHLETES CAN HELP OTHER PEOPLE THROUGH SHARING AND STORYTELLING.

Individuals can engage in NIL activities that are consistent with the law where their college is located.

The Name, Image, and Likeness legislation implemented in 2021 is somewhat of a prerequisite for challenging athletes to think outside of sports.[2] It creates an opportunity for athletes to monetize their name and image and prompts them to start establishing a future for themselves. NIL can bring forth opportunities that can set athletes on an upward financial trajectory.

Athletes, understand you are a walking brand. Whether you receive an NIL deal or not, the experience is preparing you to become a business owner, entrepreneur, author, general manager, coach, principal, athlete, or an administrator. The list is endless.

---

2 Hosick, Michelle. "NCAA adopts interim name, image, likeness policy". National College Athletic Association, 30 June 2021, https://www.ncaa.org/news/2021/6/30/ncaa-adopts-interim-name-image-and-likeness-policy.aspx

BALANCING ACT

We have covered how the development of the whole athlete can balloon into prominent monetary gains. Individuals must be in a productive mindset to be able to create, inspire, and live a wholesome life. Athletes are in a great position to build on what they already know.

Focus on establishing healthy eating habits. It is critical to learn and expand knowledge outside of sports. Providing athletes with ways to make money from the fruits of their labor is great, but we all know it takes being a well-rounded individual to gain favorable results on the playing field.

There are pressures athletes will face in college and after-college sports as well. Going to class, practice, and traveling, on top of late-night studying, are just the beginning of what student-athletes go through. Not to mention family life back home, relationships, and avoiding or working through injuries. All these things can take a toll on anyone. Foster an environment for yourself to be able to produce effectively. To represent yourself through products, building helpful habits is key.

Developing a holistic approach to help maximize your athletic prowess can be an asset for athletes. It was intriguing to hear a few of my players' stances on handling life as an athlete.

One player stated, "I find quiet time for myself and draw; it helps me regroup."

Another player expressed, "I usually treat myself to a meal at a restaurant, then go for a walk."

Simple practices allow athletes to decompress and focus on tasks and responsibilities ahead of them. The mental health aspect is just as important as weight training practices. It all intertwines. Developing healthy habits during your playing career will carry over into the next stage of your life.

After leaving basketball, there was a period where I struggled to adjust to life. It wasn't until I thought back to my time as a college athlete. It caused me to start holding myself accountable again. I concentrated on consistency with my daily routine. I thank God for self-accountability.

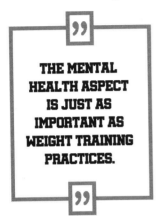

THE MENTAL HEALTH ASPECT IS JUST AS IMPORTANT AS WEIGHT TRAINING PRACTICES.

I coined the principles I use the "Go Beyond Approach" and began implementing them at the beginning of Summer 2013. I still use them to this day.

THE GO BEYOND APPROACH

- Prioritize your time. Decrease your accessibility to people to a minimum when needed. It takes time to accomplish anything. I believe it is fine to be somewhat selfish with your time.
- Find quiet time for yourself. You need time to think and reflect. As I speak about in my book, *Go Beyond: Intimate Perspectives from Former Athletes on How to Win at Life*, walking was therapeutic and still is today.
- Change your diet. When I embarked on the journey of eating a plant-based diet, it prompted me to make better decisions for my life. In addition, changing my diet was a catalyst for me to care about other areas of my life.
- Get rid of the victim mentality and face obstacles head-on.
- Operate with humility. This does not equate to acting docile and seeing yourself as inferior to others. On the contrary, by operating with humility, doors will open for you. It is about respect as well as appreciation.

- Read more! Read a variety of literature. You can gather knowledge from reading multiple genres. When you digest different perspectives, you're learning.

I needed structure. I was responsible for that in my life. It was up to me to utilize the skills and traits learned through athletics in my life, which led to coaching for me. The opportunity to serve the next range of women basketball players is what I have been doing, not knowing that coaching would lead me to becoming an author.

As an author, I can reach a surplus number of athletes from different sports. It is another avenue to serve others and create another stream of income. Educating athletes is a various approach. Each person learns differently. As you evolve, continue to set aside time for your health.

Find joy in the process. It is rewarding. Your experiences have made you who you are as an athlete. Create and execute your game plan in the next chapter of life so you can raise your level of thinking. Wealth and abundance shouldn't just revolve around money. Other areas in your life must also align with the purpose being pursued. Those positive habits create a passageway to true wealth. We have the blueprint; athletes understand the wealth standard.

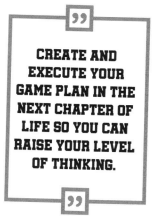

> CREATE AND EXECUTE YOUR GAME PLAN IN THE NEXT CHAPTER OF LIFE SO YOU CAN RAISE YOUR LEVEL OF THINKING.

ABOUT KEZIA

A native of Tallahassee, Florida, Kezia Conyers has over ten years of coaching at the collegiate level. Through her tenure as a coach, she has produced student-athletes who have excelled on and off the court. Many of her players have received all-conference honors and all-academic honors.

Kezia is the founder of Go Beyond Sports Network, an organization for athletes that provides comfort to those coping with discovering their ultimate identity beyond athletics through multimedia. It is a platform for athletes, coaches, administrators, and creators to connect and share knowledge, ideas, and insight on copious topics.

Kezia is a three-time author of *Go Beyond: Intimate Perspectives from Former Athletes on How to Win at Life, Go Beyond Part 2: The Next Play*, and *Coaching from the Heart: The Greatest Untold Stories*.

As a former player and collegiate coach, Kezia focuses on connecting with athletes across the spectrum by providing insight on transitioning into life after sports. She is a graduate of Appalachian State University, where she received her Bachelor of Science degree in Criminal Justice. Kezia also received her Masters of Science degree from Ohio University in Recreation and Sports Sciences.

CHAPTER FOUR

MAKE A CONNECTION

By Aswand Cruickshank

I can remember that moment from twenty years ago, like it was yesterday. My older sister walked into our parents' room laughing hysterically, but nothing was funny. At least not to me.

I had been sitting at the table in deep thought, gripping the pen. She looked over my shoulder to see what I was doing. I quickly covered as much of my spiral notebook as I could to keep her from seeing what I was doing. But it was too late. She discovered I was diligently writing a letter to the president about why football needed to be an Olympic sport.

Take a moment to let that image sink into your mind. A young, ten-year-old black boy who lived in the suburbs of Silver Spring, Maryland, was spending a portion of his summer vacation working on a very well-crafted, yet angry, letter to the president. We are talking about America's leader who institutes laws to provide jobs and end poverty.

Of course, there were far more important things to address, but nothing else mattered. I found my acceptance as a football player; it gave me a sense of identity. The area in which I grew up is known for producing the best basketball players. Kevin Durant, Victor Oladipo, Rudy Gay. Just to name a few.

I was trash at basketball. I couldn't dribble, I couldn't shoot, and I didn't have the natural athletic ability that the game required. So, seeing basketball on TV during the summer, made me feel left out, especially since the games were being played during our summer vacation and football had yet to start.

Even as a ten-year-old boy, I had a desire to take initiative on things I felt strongly about, and taking initiative is one of the key elements needed to make and hopefully exceed a six-figure salary. Another more important element? *Make a Connection*. There was no way I could have foreseen how much that experience I had writing a letter to the president was going to dictate how I live my life, and how I make my living as an adult. Constantly reaching out to schools, businesses, nonprofit organizations, trying to get booked to speak and deliver workshops.

Growing up on the outskirts of Washington, D.C., I was blessed to witness countless successful and inspiring stories about entrepreneurship. I heard so many stories that I even started my own sports franchises when I was nine years old. I'd go around the house talking about the new teams I was going to start. One was named the Winners. And then I had the Stingers a week later.

Once I graduated from Stony Brook University at twenty-two years old, my heart and mind were filled with enough ambition to blow up a hot-air balloon and travel the world. I was more than ready to put all my energy into action.

Three years after graduation, I attempted to start a minor league football organization named the "Ocean City Sharks". I chose to locate that team at the University of Maryland Eastern Shore.

The vision I had for this organization was to be a team that serves as a Farm System for the NFL. My initial career plan was to become a scout for one of the National Football League franchises, but this was the year of the NFL Lockout, the longest work stoppage in NFL history. Although I had ambition, I had enough common sense to know that my superiors didn't have all the answers. Eventually I was going to need to do things *my* way. At that point in life I didn't know, what that way would be, hence the need to make connections.

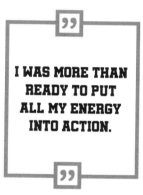

I WAS MORE THAN READY TO PUT ALL MY ENERGY INTO ACTION.

As a former football player, I did not have a realistic view of how money works. I was very confused about the difference between *money making* and *revenue generating* (which I'll discuss later in the chapter). That confusion eventually led me to hit rock bottom on multiple occasions.

Rock bottom is different for everyone. There were many nights I didn't know where I was going to sleep. I slept in my car, in parking lots around Ocean City, MD.

When I went back to Silver Spring, the car was repossessed. There I was, approaching twenty-six without transportation. I had

THERE WERE MANY NIGHTS I DIDN'T KNOW WHERE I WAS GOING TO SLEEP.

no phone. I had no income. Many nights I went to sleep hungry and heartbroken.

A lot of the things I experienced could have been avoided if I had a solid education on financial literacy and how money works. An education I *now* feel obligated to pass along to former athletes of all sports. I want to help as many people as possible avoid the pitfalls I experienced. So, here it is in three segments.

GOOD IS THE ENEMY OF GREAT

First things first, the term "Six-Figures", is something that athletes need to slowly but surely eradicate from our vocabulary. Don't get me wrong, it's a great goal to strive for, but six figures is the enemy of seven or eight figures. One phrase that comes to my mind that Jim Collins says is, "Good is the enemy of great."

Prior to my attempt to start the Ocean City Sharks, I founded a company named Gym44 Consulting (eventually it would become Gym44 Recruiting). The way Gym44 works is simple.

A coach creates an account just like you'd make an email or Facebook account. Then the coach simply posts tryouts. The incentive to *posting*, tryouts on Gym44 is the fact that each tryout has a space for advertisements. Depending on the coach, and how much traffic they can get from interested players, it could be a deciding factor in how much a business is willing to spend on ad space.

Suddenly, the idea started to work. *Worked*, as in players were reserving and requesting tryouts. I didn't want to spend too much time trying to get coaches to understand how to use Gym44, because the possibilities are actually *endless*. Meaning I didn't, and still don't (as one man) have the ability to communicate with every single coach and advertiser, about how to use Gym44 to make money. The only thing I could do was put it out there for players who were actively trying out for teams and allow things to spread via word of mouth. Therefore, I said to myself I would use Gym44 to start a team, so it can become the model

> **I WANT TO HELP AS MANY PEOPLE AS POSSIBLE AVOID THE PITFALLS I EXPERIENCED.**

franchise that other coaches and businesses can duplicate.

With that in mind, I boldly started promising potential players $5,000 to play for the Ocean City Sharks. You may be reading this and think that $5,000 is not a lot of money, but take into consideration the cost it takes to start a football team (helmets, shoulder pads, equipment, insurance, athletic trainers, etc.). The $5,000 was for each player; the roster was going to be made up of 45 players. Now, imagine a player gets injured, which is inevitable when you're talking tackle football. In the case of an injury, I would have still needed to pay the player, and go recruit another player, and pay him another $5,000. These are just the on-the-field costs. I didn't take into consideration how much it would've cost to have the players stay in a hotel for the season, and how much it would've cost to make sure they were fed. Football Players EAT. (A lot).

I was blinded by my own ambition. Former coaches warned me not to proceed. They understood the need for the NFL to have a system. While they were very impressed with my drive and ambition, financially they knew there was no way I was going to make this work by myself. But I didn't want to hear it, because I knew Gym44 gave me a way of making money, and I knew the players would show up.

The Ocean City Sharks were supposed to just be a spring league football team. Then I pushed it back into the fall. The more players who showed interest, the quicker word got around I didn't have the money I was promising to pay the players. My reputation became tarnished among the very players I wanted so badly to help. They

I WAS BLINDED BY MY OWN AMBITION.

realized my plan for how I was going to pay them wasn't fully developed, and for a football player trying to make the NFL, there is only a tiny window of opportunity.

Just so you have a visual of how committed I was to making this idea work, here is a rough timeline. I quit my job that winter. I began actively working full-time to get sponsors through the spring and summer until the entire idea became so overwhelming. At that point, my phone was cut off because I had no way of paying the bill. Players were trying to find out how, when, or even if they'd be getting paid as the fall was approaching, and NFL camps were starting up (remember I was telling the players it was going to be a farm system for the NFL, so I tried to model the process by the way the NFL teams did things).

I slept in my car for the entire year. If you were to add up all the nights I slept in a car, including my relocation to Florida, it would probably come out to almost three years.

My biggest mistake? I was thinking too small. Think about it. My goal for after college was to work in the NFL, and be in an environment with elite talent, the best of the best. Instead, I started a semi-pro team which attracted mediocre players, although attempting to start a semi-pro team displays a lot of ambition. I put the message out there as if it was going to be a team that followed

NFL guidelines, which made the dream too small for me. At twenty-four years old, my focus should have been to work for an NFL team, learn the do's and don'ts behind the scenes, develop some friendships, start a family, and then put the Ocean City Sharks together.

My actions were good. Great would have been to be patient and wait until I either raised the money or had a solid financial foundation for the team before I moved forward and started recruiting players.

My challenge to you is to take your time. As great as a six-figure salary sounds, take into consideration that the job can take up so much of your time that it prevents you from starting a business that creates eight figures. Just like the idea of me owning a team got in the way of me becoming an NFL scout.

THE DIFFERENCE BETWEEN "MONEY MAKING" AND "REVENUE GENERATING"

It was time for me to bounce back. Going broke and hitting rock bottom sucks. But, if used correctly, it can be the best thing that happens to a person. I was determined to make it something I can look back on and use it as fuel to forge ahead. I only have a chapter to share, so I won't go into all the details of my bounce back, but I'll tell you the main thing you need to hear. Take notice!

When you're making connections, you will recognize the subtle differences between entities that work for a profit and organizations that simply generate revenue because of popularity. Therefore, it's essential you notice the difference, because that difference creates the need for people like you (or me) who want to be a part of something they truly believe in.

Nike is a for-profit business. They create products that consumers buy, and they make a profit. However, the University of Alabama football program is revenue-generating. The primary focus of the program is to win championships, not make money.

The revenue is generated through fans, ticket sales, merchandise sales, and sponsorship. It's the connection between fans, or in this case, boosters or alumni, that leads to tickets being bought and merchandise being sold. When you have a revenue-generating operation, it makes for-profit businesses partner with you. Nike is a sponsor for the University of Alabama.

That's just one example. I could literally fill this entire book with examples of how connections lead to jobs being created for former athletes, just like you and my fellow contributing authors.

When I was in the process of bouncing back from my fall in Ocean City, I strategically applied for jobs where I could make a connection. Being from Maryland, the story of how Under Armour got started has always resonated with me.

I spent years thinking the founder of the company was a guy from the commercials. A ripped, black guy that either didn't make it to the NFL or recently retired. It wasn't until I reached out and sent a pitch to the company to be a sponsor for the Ocean City Sharks that I realized Kevin Plank is the founder. He was born and raised in the same neighborhood as me.

There was a time when I worked for a fitness studio in Owings Mills, Maryland. I decided to work there for two reasons. First, the studio was located a few miles from the Baltimore Ravens Practice Facility, a facility that Under Armour bought and renamed the Under

Armour Performance Center. I hoped to rub shoulders with some of the Baltimore Ravens Executives, and either try to solicit myself for a scouting job or see if I could find an angel investor for the Ocean City Sharks.

The next reason was because the studio was a "Krav Maga" studio. I wanted to learn how to teach people the art of self-defense and hand-quickness so I could add it to my skill set. The owner of the Krav Maga studio actually told me stories (during the interview) of working with some of the Baltimore Ravens tight ends and defensive linemen to improve their hand-quickness on the field. So I thought it would be a great way to work with players.

I happened to be wearing one of the first ever shirts that Under Armour designed while I was working out. During the middle of my workout, one of the members of the studio asked me, "Hey, man! Where did you get that shirt?"

I responded, "I've had it for years. Under Armour used the football team I played for as a kid, the White Oak Warriors, in one of their commercials."

The gentlemen said, "I worked for Under Armour back when there were maybe six people working for the company. Kevin Plank told us the story of him pitching to Nike about the concept of compression T-shirts, and Nike told him it would never work."

As the words came off of his lips, I had flashbacks of sleeping out of my car, driving (my mother's car) back and forth to get to the studio in Owings Mills, and the depression I experienced because of the rejection.

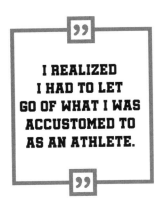

> **I REALIZED I HAD TO LET GO OF WHAT I WAS ACCUSTOMED TO AS AN ATHLETE.**

I realized I had to let go of what I was accustomed to as an athlete. I had to let go of the idea of a revenue-generating organization that created a sense of comfort and acceptance for me and put my focus on creating a money-making business.

My mindset shifted, and I began to *question how to build a* money-making company that could have a similar impact as Under Armour. How do I create an experience in which a person can see a T-shirt and it sparks up an enlightening conversation between two strangers?

I don't want to simplify this because it is *not* an easy process. You will need to make a lot of sacrifices. These will be the same sacrifices that you made as an athlete—time with friends who didn't play sports and wanted to spend all their time drinking, smoking, partying, and doing things that were not conducive to their development.

The wind sprints that you hated running, the team you played that had a player who was better than you, but you still had to compete. The time your coach screamed at you, and you had to move on to the next play.

However, just like when you played, the rewarding feeling of making progress makes it all worth it. Which takes me to segment number three. *Shift Your Focus.*

SHIFT YOUR FOCUS

As we approach our third and final segment, I'll give you some context. I left the Krav Maga studio because I decided to become a volunteer high school football coach for two seasons. I then relocated to Florida, to hit the refresh button on life.

YOU WILL NEED TO MAKE A LOT OF SACRIFICES.

As I close you out on the third segment, keep these three questions in mind:

- How will you market your business?
- How will you innovate in your business?
- How are you creating raving fans in your business?

After the football season ended, I drove from Maryland to Florida and found a job in St. Petersburg, FL, at a local fitness studio named OrangeTheory Fitness.

One day while I was at work, I was checking my email. I received a message from the Miami Dolphins Foundation. They were offering me a part-time position as a "50/50 Raffle ticket seller". My thirtieth birthday was coming, and I needed to be with an NFL team. My goal was to have a foot in the door with an NFL team by thirty.

Once I accepted the position with the Miami Dolphins, I went on another job hunt because the OrangeTheory Fitness studio was too far, and the Dolphins gig didn't pay enough. I was fortunate enough to know the type of places that would hire me on the spot. I was already accustomed to being uncomfortable so I could, and was willing to, do whatever it took to take advantage of the opportunity to work with the Miami Dolphins.

I found a fitness studio called 9Round Kickboxing and Fitness. In the back of the gym, I noticed a couch and ended up sleeping there so I could save as much money as possible. Before I go any further, please highlight, underline, write down, do whatever it is you need to do to remember:

"It's not about how much money you make,
It's about how much money you SAVE!"

I am living proof of this statement. South Florida is one of the most expensive cities to live in. Fortunately, I could get by on two part-time jobs because every cent I was making was being reinvested into my business.

Think about the plan I had for connecting the Krav Maga Studio and the Baltimore Ravens. I recreated that same vision in South Florida, with the 9Round Fitness studio and the Miami Dolphins foundation.

Eventually, I became restless with the management of both these jobs. My hiring manager with the Miami Dolphins Foundation never created or incentivized any system to follow up with fans who bought a raffle ticket on game days. I happened to be one of the top sellers and wanted a full-time position; I became very frustrated with the lack of support.

The owner at the 9Round studio continuously showed certain members more attention than others, and because I was the "lead" trainer, I had to deal with backlash that came from people leaving the gym. The pressure to make everyone else feel welcomed became unnecessary because the owner had no expansion plans.

The combination of these two circumstances forced me to become the entrepreneur I was called to be. I believe this is a facet of entrepreneurship that often gets overlooked. Sometimes, life's circumstances and things that don't go according to the plan will leave one with no option but to be an entrepreneur.

I dug into YouTube archives to rewatch inspirational videos planting seeds of optimism in my mind over the years. I'll share one with you.

"MINDSET OF A WINNER"

By Seth Godin, Best-selling Author

Seth Godin was once asked how to avoid mediocrity. He used the example of Google and Yahoo to make his point. Seth Godin stated, "If you go to yahoo.com, there are 150 links on one page. A few years ago, if you went to Google, there were only three because Google lost opportunities to drive people to finance, weather, or whatever they were needing to search. They only did one thing. So, if someone asked which site to use, mostly everyone would say Google."

That lesson has been invaluable for me because my business is about getting total strangers to listen to a new idea as soon as we meet. In that same video, Seth Godin speaks about this idea of communicating emotionally. He specifically says, "You can only emotionally communicate with someone if they're listening."

With that understanding, I decided to put all my time and energy into becoming a full-time entrepreneur. Shortly after making that decision, I wrote my first book, titled, *Swift-LY: Your Guide to Innovative Teamwork*. Then I began hosting a podcast—*Move Swiftly: Finding Your Place in This World*. Then I wrote another book, *Make Your Move,* which shares a unique look into boxing, dance, and entrepreneurship. I even created a coloring book that aligns with my brand.

All of these things created the connection for me to write a chapter for this book. I've already made more connections just by showing up and committing to being a part of *Six-Figure Athlete*. Everything began with the intention of making a connection with someone I didn't know.

> YOU CAN ONLY EMOTIONALLY COMMUNICATE WITH SOMEONE IF THEY'RE LISTENING.

A few months before the coronavirus pandemic shut us down, I attended Unleash the Power Within, a live Tony Robbins event in Miami, Florida. It was there that I discovered the same three questions I asked you to ponder on.

How will you market your business?

1. Marketing: Remember, it wasn't until I grew up that I realized the founder of Under Armour was Kevin Plank, not the former athlete he paid to wear his product in commercials. That's marketing done correctly. The founder stays in his lane as the creator of the product and allows others to do their job.

When I started Gym44.com, it wasn't about making money. It was about getting coaches who've been around longer than me to post a tryout. It has become my job to figure out how to create the revenue stream for it.

How will you innovate in your business?

2. Innovation: Kevin Plank is on record saying he doesn't own the patents for tight, stretchy t-shirts. He says, "We launched with that product and grew from there."

I don't own the patents for the word "Swift-LY" or "Make Your Move". I was just able to tweak those words and use phrases that attract the coaches and players I'm striving to serve every day.

How are you creating raving fans in your business?

3. Create Raving Fans: Stephen Curry, Tom Brady, Ray Lewis, Michael Phelps, Dwayne 'The Rock' Johnson, and Misty Copeland are just a few of the athletes who Under Armour has sponsored. We could fill an entire page (or two) if we listed all of them.

Another example is Beats By Dre. Before it was sold to Apple, Dr. Dre gave famous athletes points in the company. Once he sold to Apple, the athletes who invested got a payout.

In my business, the fans are the many people I've had uplifting conversations with at the gym, sold raffle tickets to at the Miami Dolphins games, and the parents and students I'm around every day as a current teacher.

As a former (or current) athlete, there will be opportunities to exceed six figures. It doesn't make you selfish or arrogant to want to make more money. There is a standard you have grown accustomed to, and you have the discipline to take full advantage of every opportunity you get.

Your time as an athlete goes by very fast. Thinking about what's next is always a challenge; however, your response to challenges will determine where you end up in the future. Go *Make a Connection*.

ABOUT ASWAND

Aswand Cruickshank is a multi-published author and podcast host. He started playing football at the age of seven, and the lessons he has learned from his fifteen years as a player have played a major role in every decision he has made as an adult.

Aswand had the unique opportunity to play under coaches that had a tremendous amount of respect and influence, simply based on the fact that these men had no interest in leaving (for "better jobs").

After graduating from Stony Brook University, he became an independent scout for National Scouting Report, while also working as a sales consultant for several fitness brands.

He started his own scouting company named, Gym44 Recruiting, and spent two seasons as a volunteer high school football coach for Blake High School in Silver Spring, Maryland. Aswand relocated to South Florida to work for the Miami Dolphins Foundation and now has a mission to use sports to teach young people all the life lessons his coaches taught him.

Also, tune into the "Move Swiftly Podcast", a show he uses as a way of teaching people how to find their place in this world.

IG: @Swift_ly44

FaceBook: Aswand Cruickshank

LinkedIN: Aswand Cruickshank

Podcast: Move Swiftly

CHAPTER FIVE

WHEN PREPARATION MEETS OPPORTUNITY

By Taj Dashaun

With a sigh of relief and trepidation, I turned my two-weeks notice in to my boss. There was no turning back now. My parents thought I was crazy for leaving a comfortable salary as a corporate recruiter to focus on my side-hustle. Maybe I was. My side-hustle was an emerging company that helped athletes in their transition into life after sports.

Based on the concept of "thriving, not just surviving", I named my coaching business Thrive After Sports.

After quitting that job, I quickly burned through my savings and then did the unthinkable—I asked my parents to move back in with them.

Despite their initial shock, my parents believed in me enough to allow me to move back home while I focused on bringing my vision to life.

Things were moving slowly with Thrive After Sports during the first two years, so I picked up a part-time job along the way to cover my expenses.

The last part-time job I had before going full-time with Thrive After Sports was as a glass installer. There I was, a college graduate, with five years of sales, recruiting, and account management experience under my belt, installing shower glass and bath enclosures for fifteen dollars an hour.

I knew I was overqualified, but I needed a job, so who was I to complain? I was determined to make my business work by any means.

I actually enjoyed the glass installation job because it allowed me to drive around every day with a team of guys, going into people's homes in upscale neighborhoods. I got to experience the same brotherhood of being in the locker room, while having the flexibility to take days off and carve out time to work on my business. Plus, I didn't have to sit in an office, staring at the clock and waiting to go home like I did in previous jobs.

Doing manual labor made it easy for me to come home from work and use my mental faculties to keep building. Even though my body was tired after a long day of work, my mind was still sharp.

One day, I was listening to a podcast as I was driving to install some glass. This wasn't anything out of the norm. I constantly listened to podcasts to help expand my business acumen.

Right as I arrived on location, the words from the podcast host stopped me dead in my tracks.

"Sometimes your story won't pan out exactly the way you plan it, but if you keep an open mind, it could turn out even better."

I pulled into a parking spot. Looking down at my phone, I pushed pause. I needed to process what I had just heard. My car was silent with only the distant chatter of people outside, but the words he had just said were on repeat.

Slowly inhaling, I closed my eyes. The words were clearer than the glass I had been installing for almost a year at this point.

So focused on my thoughts, I didn't even notice what was going on around me. As I skimmed my surroundings, everyone seemed to be so happy. I heard laughter and witnessed people smiling. Some were riding bikes and enjoying the warm California sunshine. And here I was, getting ready to clock in to install glass for another twelve-hour shift.

I KNEW I WANTED MORE, AND I WAS GETTING IMPATIENT.

Something inside me that day wouldn't let those words go. I knew I wanted more, and I was getting impatient.

Did I want to spend the rest of my life installing glass? *Hell no!* It was only a temporary situation to help me take care of expenses while I continued to build. However, there was a fear inside of me as I slowly approached the age of thirty that I would be stuck doing part-time jobs forever, and my business would never be profitable enough for me to work with former athletes full-time. Fear began to creep in and made its presence known.

I didn't want to let my parents down. I didn't want to let myself down. I didn't want to watch all the hard work I had put in over the years result in a mediocre life. What I didn't realize was the chain of events that were unfolding led me to some unexpected opportunities that would change the trajectory of my life forever.

> **FEAR BEGAN TO CREEP IN AND MADE ITS PRESENCE KNOWN.**

I had already lived every athlete's worst nightmare: transitioning into the real (working) world with no game plan and no clarity about what the next chapter held for me. Now I was determined to help other athletes like myself get through that transition.

When entering the workforce (or entrepreneurship), you're joining a new team. Except now, you're last on the depth chart. You go from being at the top of your field in your sport, to starting out at the bottom of the totem pole in your post-sport life. You have to work hard and climb your way up, which can be challenging and frustrating in the beginning.

If you're able to stay disciplined, gain experience, and continue to persevere, you'll naturally break away and become the star player you once were.

The question that stumps so many former athletes remains: "What do I do next?" I had been there for quite some time. I didn't want to settle.

Thankfully, I was actually still coaching several clients with Thrive After Sports when I began the glass installation job. I spent as much time as I could work on my business so I could earn a steady income and be a full-time entrepreneur. The stream of income I thought I would bring in became more like a dripping faucet—with frozen pipes.

During a session with one of my clients, they mentioned wanting to write a book. That's all I needed to hear. I went on a search to help them. I had never written a book before, so I began researching to see how I could assist. After all, one of things I enjoy doing most is helping people.

I reached out to a friend who mentioned in passing she'd worked with a publishing company several years ago. Her book was very professionally done, so I figured I'd ask her who she worked with. She was eager to share the company's contact information. She spoke to the great service and how they could help publish my client's book with ease.

I reached out to the founder of Self-Publish-N-30-Days, Mr. Darren M. Palmer, on LinkedIn. After sending a few messages back and forth, we connected on a consultation and began discussing my client publishing a book, but the conversation quickly shifted into talking about my business.

Darren was very blunt with me, which I appreciated. He talked to me like a football coach. After telling him about some of the challenges I was facing with getting my business off the ground, he made it very clear I needed help positioning myself for better success.

Over the next few months, Darren became the coach and mentor I needed. He understood exactly what I was trying to do and how I could be more strategic in my approach while reaching more people.

Not only did Darren become my mentor, but he eventually extended the opportunity for me to come on board as vice president, where I could work directly with aspiring authors, connecting them with our editing, design, and marketing team to help publish their books.

I HAD FORGOTTEN THE POWER OF TEAMWORK.

Little did I know that working for Self-Publish -N- 30 Days was exactly the team I was missing when I left the world of football.

When I graduated from college, I went from being part of the tight-knit community of a football team, to trying "to figure it all out on my own". I didn't realize it at the time, but I had been trying to be the "lone wolf" for too long, and it was slowing me down. Not only was I trying to do everything by myself from a business perspective, I was also flying solo in everyday life. I had forgotten the power of teamwork.

I had also painted myself into a corner regarding the demographic I was serving. Since I started Thrive After Sports, I was limited to serving only one group of people: athletes who needed help transitioning after sports.

Working at Self-Publish -N- 30 Days has given me the opportunity to serve in a greater capacity. Now I'm not limited to just helping athletes transition. I can help athletes (and countless other individuals) tell their stories to the world.

I've been able to foster connection and collaboration between other current and former athletes, so we can all leave a trail of breadcrumbs for the athletes coming in behind us. By having a reason to collaborate, and helping others with their books, I began to see myself as the Quincy Jones, or the DJ Khaled, of the Athlete Transition space.

Bringing others together to collaborate also expanded my network and caused an exponential growth in every area of my life. At one point, I remember thinking to myself, *How did I end up working for a publishing company?* I did not have any publishing experience under my belt, but I knew how to be teachable, resilient, and open.

I threw myself whole-heartedly into this role. I spent hours learning everything I could about the world of publishing. Becoming the vice president of Self Publish -N- 30 Days catapulted my career because I chose growth and evolution. I learned things I never thought I'd be learning.

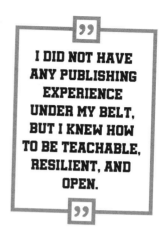

I DID NOT HAVE ANY PUBLISHING EXPERIENCE UNDER MY BELT, BUT I KNEW HOW TO BE TEACHABLE, RESILIENT, AND OPEN.

I didn't need capital or a supply chain. All I needed was me, so I got to work. I published my first book, hosted multiple podcasts, facilitated several co-authored book projects (including this one), and helped other business owners and former athletes align with their purpose.

Around the same time I connected with Darren, I also met Myriam Glez, the founder of Athletes Soul on LinkedIn. Myriam and I aligned right from the get-go. She'd seen the work I'd been doing over the years and wanted to bring me on board as a transition coach for her organization.

Boom! Another unexpected opportunity had revealed itself to me, and I had been preparing myself for it all along without even knowing it.

I can finally say I am living with purpose. I am grateful because not only is my life filled with income-earning opportunities; it is also filled with endless possibilities to serve others.

The way I look at life, as long as you strive to be the best at what you do and enjoy doing it, you'll be successful no matter what. However, it's important to remember that being "the best" takes time, which is something we former athletes often struggle with when entering the postseason of our lives.

Everyone who says, "I wish I had more opportunities," doesn't understand how opportunities truly work. An opportunity is your

I CAN FINALLY SAY I AM LIVING WITH PURPOSE.

chance to give before you get. An unmet need, for example, is an opportunity for you to step up and help someone else. The door of opportunity swings on unexpected hinges, and you must be prepared when that door swings open.

Here are some ways to find and embrace opportunities:

- Dedicate time each day to imagine the life you want to live and take action. Clarity comes to those who take action; confusion comes to the inactive.
- Join forces with someone who is already making a difference.
- Expect a lot. Bring a lot. Low standards never produce high results.
- Embrace the power of imperfect solutions. Don't worry about solving everything, just solve something.
- Always ask yourself, "What am I going to gain from the next hour?" It could be money, peace of mind, rest, relaxation, or knowledge. But when it's "nothing", you need to change your plans.

My hope is that by sharing my unconventional journey with you, you'll gain the courage to chart your own path and create your own destiny. If you apply the lessons from this book, I have no doubt you'll be well on the way to earning six figures, and much more.

The path to success isn't linear, so be ready to embrace the good, the bad, and the ugly that come your way.

It's no secret athletes love competition. We get a thrill out of going head-to-head with one another and competing to be the best. If we can learn to compete with ourselves in a healthy way, our athletic mindset will push us to keep getting better each day at anything we set our minds to.

Being an elite athlete requires dedication, discipline, and the ability to learn things quickly; take that same passion for improvement and apply it to your new arena.

If you're able to take traits like these and apply them directly to your profession of choice, there's no doubt opportunities will find you. Will you be ready?

ABOUT TAJ

Taj Dashaun is an athlete-transition coach, speaker and 3X author. He currently serves as the vice president for Self Publish -N- 30 Days.

As a former Division I college football player for Stony Brook University, when his football career ended, Taj struggled heavily with depression. Because he was so focused on the game, he never fully developed a clear vision for his life.

After several years of stumbling around in the emotional darkness of uncertainty, Taj began to take his eyes off of himself and focus on serving others. He now runs Thrive After Sports, an intensive program for retired athletes who, like he once was, are struggling to adapt to life after sports. Not only does Taj help former players land jobs and start businesses, he helps them find fulfillment in their lives.

It's become his personal mission and passion to reach out and help others overcome the fear, frustration, and uncertainty associated with life post-athletics. Taj is also the host of the *Thrive After Sports* podcast.

To connect with Taj and learn more, visit www.tajdashaun.com. Taj can also be found on Instagram and LinkedIn @tajdashaun and Facebook @coachtajdashaun.

CHAPTER SIX

A BRIDGE OF HOPE

By Brice Kassa

Wisdom and integrity shapes excellence. Wisdom is the supreme evidence that walking the path God sets before us brings success. Thank God He is doing great things in our lives. He has given us dreams to fulfill, and dreams transcend our identity.

By sharing my struggles and some key experiences in my life, I want to encourage others to tap into their purpose and be determined to persevere. My relationship with God has gotten me through perilous times. With a renewed sense of hope in humanity, people are fighting to make a difference in the world.

As a former basketball player in Gabon, Africa, (located between Cameroon and Congo) my mission in life is to help people over an obstacle by providing a route that would otherwise be impossible; hence, a Bridge of Hope.

This effort was inspired by the difficulty I faced attempting to achieve my dream of playing basketball in the US.

It was hard, and I thought I had the talent and qualities to make it, so I questioned God. Why am I trapped here like this? I felt abandoned, rejected, and misunderstood. Eventually, I began searching for the good in people.

Instead of submerging myself in my emotions, I decided to consider the advice of people who cared for me. I watched a video about Michael Jordan. Here was the greatest basketball player of all time, speaking openly about his weaknesses. I thought to myself, *Who am I not to consider my shortcomings if I truly wanted to go higher?* I have to be transparent and accept that changes have to be made.

Out of my willingness to mature, I set my sights on a different goal for the moment–helping others: younger, talented players who had the potential to make it quicker than me.

We fight against "crumb-settling", or accepting less than we desire, to reach financial freedom and the ability to take care of our families. Many struggle in my country, so it has always been my priority to help my family and those I care about.

My love of basketball began when I was eleven years old. I was introduced to the sport when I saw a schoolmate performing some fancy moves during PE class. I was so intrigued, I asked him if he could teach me to do the same thing.

The next day, he took me to his house after school and showed me the most amazing thing I had ever seen—a showcase of VHS tapes and posters of Shaquille O'Neal and Alonzo Mourning gracing his bedroom wall. He let me borrow a VHS tape featuring Magic Johnson. I was so intrigued by his personality and smile. From that day on, my dream was to make it to the NBA and play for the Lakers.

Some of my best memories occurred on the basketball court. You would rarely see me without a ball in hand. I was so thankful to God for my abilities and every opportunity I had to play. It felt so good to shoot. I had that same feeling when I helped someone. I felt as if the sky had opened up and anything was possible. There was a sense of freedom, and all the stresses of life melted away as if I were listening to my favorite song.

It was this love, passion, and dedication I had for the game that I dreamed would help me create a better future for myself and my family. So, I hoped. I prayed, and I played from 1995 all the way to 2019. It never occurred to me how financially difficult it would be. I thought all those years I would get money, go to the US, and come back to my country as a wealthy man. Then, I could take care of my family, run my businesses, and help many people. I always had this in mind; however, it was far from the reality I lived daily.

From 1995 to 2000, I earned $14 a month playing basketball. I practiced three days a week, running under the sun, and losing and winning games on the weekends.

I lived at home with my family—my mother and father, two brothers, and two sisters. My dad worked for the government and my mother worked at home as a tailor. We lived in Libreville, the capital city of Gabon. My dad raised us on his own salary with no businesses on the side.

I didn't have to worry about housing in my early career because my father allowed me to stay at home. It wasn't easy for him. He struggled to pay for our schooling, buy food for the family, and take care of our needs. I wasn't happy to live in that situation.

I wanted to persevere and hopefully make it to the US, but the $14 I had was only enough to pay for transportation back and forth from home to the basketball court.

I WAS SO THANKFUL TO GOD FOR MY ABILITIES AND EVERY OPPORTUNITY I HAD TO PLAY.

In 2001, I played in two other basketball clubs. Again, only earning $14 a month. I did this until 2008. I continued to live with my family. During this time, I had to walk from home to the university for practice, which was about 40 kilometers or 25 miles.

It became difficult for me to eat because my father had lost his job for a while. For many months, we had meals of sardines and rice—no meat. Since my dad couldn't provide food, he would say to me, "Brice, stop dreaming about basketball. You dream too much. Find a job and grow up."

I had to find a job. Fortunately, a good friend of mine, was able to secure me a five-month contract with a flight company. I was with a team of four people who took care of the needs of travelers coming from all around the world. Part of my job was being an aircraft marshal, where I used high-visibility paddles to guide airplanes to runway ramps. I earned $200 per month, which helped my family with food, but it took away from my time to practice basketball. I started to believe I would forget my dreams of going to the NBA and pursue my aviation career.

Unfortunately, the company shut down, leaving me jobless and making life extremely hard again. I finished the season with the basketball club with the same $14-a-month salary.

From 2009 to 2019, I played for several other basketball clubs. They provided housing, and the salaries were a little better. I earned $125 a month to play. It was a good salary, but we still were not paid regularly.

We played the entire season two times and received no pay. The club blamed it on business and administration failures. Here, I was in a situation where I had the opportunity to win championships and make plans for my life, but was forced to sacrifice by going hungry every day.

I went to practice mornings, afternoons, and nights. Sometimes, I would find coins or bills on the ground, which I would use for food. I also had to borrow money when it became too hard for me.

I thank God for the people who helped me buy medicine when I got sick. During these hard times, I always knew inside of me I was created for a greater purpose than myself. God made me for His universal purposes to give hope to others and help them achieve a better life. In 2015, I felt I was on the verge of doing just this. I was the fifth-best scorer in my country, and I had made a name for myself, shooting threes.

I received an invitational letter to play with the national team that would later go to the well-known Afrobasket Tournament. This tournament offered many opportunities to play in other countries, including the US. I was one of twenty-six players who would practice together for two months before the final cuts were made. Unfortunately, I didn't make that last cut. It was tough, but I persevered, playing for four more years and setting my country's record for the most three-pointers made in a game.

Ephesians 1:11 says, "In Him, we were also chosen having been predestined according to the plan of Him who works out everything in conformity with the purpose of His will." That is why I believe sharing my testimony will impact nations.

When I talk about helping people become better, God revealed to me three specific areas to teach:

1. Basketball players improve their shooting skills.
2. Non-English speakers learn the language.
3. Athletes learn how to take care of themselves mentally and persevere through challenges.

I had personal experience in these three areas, so I knew how important they were to have as an aspiring player in my country. I

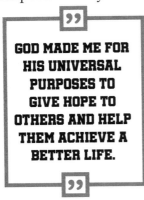

GOD MADE ME FOR HIS UNIVERSAL PURPOSES TO GIVE HOPE TO OTHERS AND HELP THEM ACHIEVE A BETTER LIFE.

found that other players had the same problems, and I realized that not being proficient in these areas could prevent a player from reaching his goals.

When I played, I built wonderful friendships, formed bonds of brotherhood with my teammates and established good communication with the team's management. It wasn't always perfect, but I had the best interest of my teammates in mind.

I made it my responsibility to help them with their shooting form, boost their confidence, and mentor them by teaching them how to understand the game and be resilient. I made myself available any time of the day to work with players in need of help.

I wanted to give them the help I never received as a young player. Helping others gave me the strength to help myself. It helped to heal my heart. I wanted to instill the passion and drive for basketball the same way my friend did the first time I saw him playing basketball.

When I was younger, my dad told my brothers and me he would always manage himself, so we would never go hungry. That our basic needs would always be met. He instilled in me a desire to help when I perceived a need. That foundation followed me past my upbringing. Above that, God gave that assignment of giving to my grandfather, who passed that down to my father, who then left me the same legacy.

I downloaded workout videos and made recordings of my teammates to post on social media and give to scouts and recruits. I did this for many players in my country, hoping to see them achieve success in their own careers. One of my first mentees was Therence Mayimba. He is a cousin from my father's side who I met in Port Gentil in 2009 while playing for an elite basketball club in Gabon, Stade Mandji.

> HELPING OTHERS GAVE ME THE STRENGTH TO HELP MYSELF.

Therence was a young, talented, and ambitious player. He was working hard to care for his ailing mother, and I knew he needed a safe environment to grow and develop his skills. He moved in with me, and I took responsibility for him as a big brother. I introduced him to the Internet and showed him how to record and edit video footage.

We worked on basketball fundamentals and found training and videos online to help sharpen his skills. We had long conversations about God and spiritual development, and I always told him he could succeed in life and reach his dreams.

Therence ended up going to the United States in 2011 to attend Montrose Christian School in Rockville, Maryland. He later became the 9th best prospect in the state and received offers from many NCAA Division I basketball programs. He currently plays for Aix Vennelles basketball club in France. Therence recently told me how valuable my mentorship had been in his life and even the impact it continues to make.

Along with my basketball career, I have also been an English teacher for secondary and high school students in my country. It has been another platform for me to use my gifts and talents. I also had to update my English skills by meeting with more experienced teachers in the field who gave me suggestions and materials to help me improve.

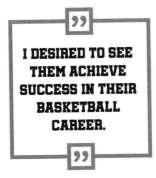

I DESIRED TO SEE THEM ACHIEVE SUCCESS IN THEIR BASKETBALL CAREER.

I set up English clubs in the schools that helped students speak English fluently and become successful on the national examinations. I provided the same level of dedication to all my students. From the most challenged students who didn't understand a word of English to the top students in my class-those ready for the next level.

I was patient and dedicated while also challenging myself and my students. It was an exciting experience that gave us both substantial rewards. During classes, I could truly perceive the desire of these young students to understand the lessons. Our time together was a time for commitment, vocation, and devotion.

I was there not only to instruct, but to motivate, correct, discipline, and provide the Word of God and His wisdom to help the students achieve their goals. Many students didn't want to miss my class because they had such horrendous home lives. They told me my class gave them hope. Students came to believe that all things were possible. The Bible says, in I Peter 4:19, "Those who suffer according to God's will should commit themselves to their faithful Creator and continue to do good."

As an English professor and basketball player, trainer, and mentor, my job inspired me to begin the FeatMaster Academy project.

My aim in the project is to help players internationally develop their basketball and English skills and improve their mental fortitude throughout the game and in life.

Since God also blessed me with the gift of drawing, I have been able to create the blueprints for a facility that would house FeatMaster Academy. It will be a community bigger than life; not only about basketball, but a community of investors who understand the value of sowing seeds in the lives of others. It's about identifying needs and providing solutions and results that impact generations to come. FeatMaster Academy will provide benefits for players that will improve the quality of their lives mentally, physically, and spiritually, so that no player leaves unchanged. The building will be equipped with classrooms, a gymnasium, and a cafeteria, as well as living quarters. Players will be able to come from all over the world and receive the highest level of basketball training.

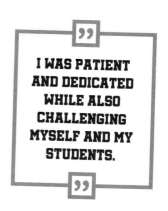

I WAS PATIENT AND DEDICATED WHILE ALSO CHALLENGING MYSELF AND MY STUDENTS.

Classes will be provided for those who need to learn or improve their English reading, writing, comprehension, and speaking skills. We will also provide mental health resources, legal consultation, and on-site trainers to address any physical concerns and make sure that players are in optimal shape for performance.

Another very important aspect of FeatMaster Academy will address the spiritual health of players and provide an environment that creates a sense of community. Players will be encouraged to know the Creator and understand the purpose He has given them upon this earth. They will then be able to seek wisdom and apply the revelation from God to their lives.

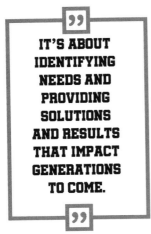

> **IT'S ABOUT IDENTIFYING NEEDS AND PROVIDING SOLUTIONS AND RESULTS THAT IMPACT GENERATIONS TO COME.**

At the end of the day, the wisdom of God's Word will always sustain the world. Proverbs 4:5 says, "Get wisdom; get understanding," and verse 11 says, "I guide you in the way of wisdom and lead you along straight paths." This is the foundation of every player's success. Players will have the opportunity to attend bible study classes, Sunday worship services, and teachings led by guest ministers, pastors, and evangelists.

By serving its participants as basketball players and unique individuals, FeatMaster Academy will provide a life-altering experience that will equip players to go out and impact the world around them.

I am currently building a network of coaches, managers, trainers, and players from around the world who will help FeatMaster Academy become a global success. Above all, I am most confident that, as God placed the vision within me, He will undoubtedly bring it to pass.

God truly has plans for each of us, and everyone has access to the revelation by God about their skills, abilities, and talents. Your talents will set you free from the bondage of ignorance and unfaithfulness towards God. I Peter 4:10-11 says, "Each one should use whatever gift he has received to serve others, faithfully administering God's grace in various forms. If any speaks, he should do it as one, speaking the very words of God. If anyone serves., he should do it with the strength God provides so that God may be praised through Jesus Christ in all things. To Him be the glory and the power forever and ever. Amen."

We make a difference in people's lives by holding on to the greatest legacy ever—which is love. A life without love cannot be productive. It is loving God by knowing Him, answering His call, loving yourself, loving your gifts, and loving people around you. It is not a simple task, but truly, not impossible. God made me a compassionate person—confident, resilient, and a team player with strong leadership and mentorship abilities.

My life experiences of basketball struggles, hardships, and instability forced me to hold on to God's call. I've understood that He cares more than anyone possibly could. I survived through His grace, having faith in His promises and consistency in His Word. He protected and comforted me even until now.I never knew that one day, He would ask me to take part in the writing of an international project. Our sons, daughters, brothers, and sisters in Gabon, America, and around the world will be blessed by the gems of experiences. I wish to end by saying that wisdom from God's Word, love, and skills mastered are the foundation of making six figures.

As God's creation, we sow hope into people's lives, and we will reap blessings, a bountiful harvest from God. Proverbs 24:14 says, "Know also that wisdom is sweet to your soul. If you find it, there is a future hope for you, and your hope will not be cut off."

A LIFE WITHOUT LOVE CANNOT BE PRODUCTIVE.

We must continue to help one another with projects like this that can change the narrative of those many players around the world who struggle daily to have their basic needs met. I believe everyone in this book will provide value to help former athletes monetize their skills.

Let's keep our relationship with God so He may give us the revelation of our skills. In this, we follow the divine connections that will change our lives forever. In one of my favorite books, *The Purpose Driven Life*, author Rick Warren says, "The way you see your life shapes your life. How you define life determines your destiny. Your perspective will influence how you invest your time, spend your money, use your talents, and value your relationships" (Rick Warren, 2002).

"Know also that wisdom is sweet to your soul. If you find it, there is a future hope for you, and your hope will not be cut off."
— Proverbs 24:14

ABOUT BRICE

Brice Kassa is an author, writer, speaker, entrepreneur, and founder of FeatMaster Academy. After graduating from high school in 2004, he enrolled in Omar Bongo University of Libreville. Throughout his life, Brice played for several well-known organizations in the country, even into his 30s. He still holds the country's title for the most three-pointers made in a game.

From reading books to studying online, Brice learned about entrepreneurship, business, and leadership. Filled with ambition, he always found a way to exercise his entrepreneurial spirit, whether by starting English clubs in high schools or gathering together young players for skill and development sessions.

With an excellent background in the English language, Brice also teaches at local high schools. He assists younger players to improve their basketball skills and shares with them many lessons he has learned in life. In his spare time, he sells his artwork and pursues his love of writing.

He currently lives in Libreville, Gabon, where he works diligently on bringing the plans of FeatMaster Academy to fulfillment. He continues to pursue his dreams and make a difference in the lives of those he encounters.

CHAPTER SEVEN

AN INTROVERT IN THE SPORTS INDUSTRY

By Michelle Meyer

W hen I received a meeting request from the CEO of a leading company in my industry, I was ecstatic. My startup, NIL Network, was still in its infancy stages. I wasn't yet looking to monetize and was just focusing on building the brand and creating a community in the new billion-dollar industry known as Name, Image, and Likeness (NIL).

This new industry developed overnight when the NCAA abruptly changed its outdated policy around amateurism and permitted all 500,000 collegiate athletes to monetize their NIL. Collegiate athletes are now getting compensated through endorsement deals, brand ambassadorships, autograph sales, running camps, and launching their own businesses.

My passion project, NIL Network, was created eight months before the policy change as a hub of resources to assist athletes, coaches, and administrators in navigating this emerging industry.

And it was getting noticed.

"Come on board with us. We're building the one-stop-shop for NIL!" the CEO bellowed through the phone. "We're going to be *the* hub. No one else will compete with us. If you don't..." he trailed off.

The unspoken message was screaming through the phone: "If you don't, we are then business competitors, and your little passion project, of course, won't survive."

Apprehension quickly replaced my elation.

"Ok. Thanks for the convo. Let's chat again soon," I muttered.

Months after this conversation, I'm still thinking about it.

My startup was getting national attention? Great! My startup was on the radar and potentially threatening an established company run by an industry leader? Definitely a positive problem.

> "
> **APPREHENSION QUICKLY REPLACED MY ELATION.**
> "

But I never imagined being here a year later. What started as a passion project—*can I build a website that helps people understand the name, image, and likeness changes in collegiate sports?*—turned into a nationally recognized brand in a rapidly developing industry.

To say the NIL Network was bootstrapped is an understatement. For better or worse, I have been a one-woman team, navigating every avenue of business in the past year. Website development? Check. SEO optimization? Check. Building a social media following? Check. Navigating the business world, partnerships, and all the nuances and layers of entrepreneurship? I'll always be a work in progress.

It's fair to say I've learned more in the past year than I've learned over the past decade of my professional career. While there have been countless frustrating hours (and a few tears) spent figuring out things that have nothing to do with the core business, sometimes derailing the whole day, I wouldn't change a thing.

Working in every role in every "department" of my small business has given me a foundational understanding of the nuances and demands of each role. In addition, it's given me the confidence to push back, ask questions, and overall, find my voice as an introverted female in the male-dominated industry of the sports business.

How Did I Get Here?

Around the one-year anniversary of NIL Network, I was updating my mother on some recent business developments and upcoming opportunities I was excited about.

Her response to my excitement made me pause: "You've strived your whole life to be the best at something, to lead your peers. It seems like you've finally found your niche. I'm so proud of you."

My mother was referring to my incessant and sometimes ridiculous approach to all aspects of my life as a child. If I wasn't the best at reading, writing, math, soccer, basketball, volleyball, softball, and anything else I tried, I was not content. If I wasn't in charge of the playground activities, birthday party plans, and the sleepover schedule, I was not content. After observing me on the kindergarten playground, my father lovingly (and embarrassingly) nicknamed me "The General". It stuck.

Sports were a great avenue for me to engage in from a young age and have since been a central and consistent focus in my life. The question that is commonly asked of former collegiate and professional athletes, "How did you transition from being an athlete to your career?" never resonated with me. It wasn't an option for me. I love sports. The community, the teamwork, the competitiveness, the mindset, and the focus on attaining your goals—every part of it. I was determined to transition my athletic career into a professional one.

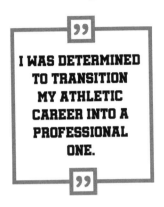

I WAS DETERMINED TO TRANSITION MY ATHLETIC CAREER INTO A PROFESSIONAL ONE.

While I do think there is a bit of luck to land a career in sports, I also think that the "luckiest" position themselves to get "lucky" and that the lessons we learn as athletes position us to get "lucky" often.

The most important lesson I've learned from sports, and something I have practiced so much it's become a personality trait, is how to shamelessly and relentlessly pursue your goals. Want to get recruited by a top-twenty volleyball program as a 5'6" defensive player from a small town? Show up consistently, train endlessly, actively take part in the recruiting process, demonstrate value to the coaching staff, and relentlessly pursue that goal.

Want to play volleyball professionally overseas in a position in which international players almost never get contracts? Data-mine 10,000 club emails across the world, send out a thousand emails with your recruiting video attached, set up tryouts across Europe for yourself, and relentlessly pursue that goal. Want to coach beach volleyball at the D1 level when it was just becoming a college sport? Call the ten programs that have beach volleyball, share your story, and when you get an offer, book the first ticket to Hawaii to coach beach volleyball at the University of Hawaii. Shameless and relentless pursuit.

From the little girl who spent nearly every free hour honing her craft to ensure earning a starting position on the top team to the woman navigating a rapidly developing industry, my mother was not wrong. I have relentlessly and unabashedly pursued my goals, whether on the court or in my professional career.

Going All-in on Myself: Creating NIL Network

The most challenging thing I've ever done is solo entrepreneurship. Every pivot, every strategy, every partnership, and all the moves I've made have taken an immense amount of courage to overcome the fear of the unknown. I've learned to be brave, trust my instincts, and realize that as long as the decisions I'm making are in line with my values, I can't go too wrong.

I've never done anything so demanding, and yet, so enjoyable. And I have never been more determined to succeed. So, how did I plant myself in the middle of this industry?

Name. Image. Likeness. The first time I heard those three words strung together was during the O'Bannon trial. At the time, I was in my first Division 1 position, coaching beach volleyball at the University of Hawaii. I knew that this decision would have massive implications for decades to come.

Over the next few years, numerous lawsuits were brought against the NCAA. There was a growing movement of student-athlete empowerment, and anyone monitoring the landscape could see that something had to give.

In 2019, California passed legislation (SB206) requiring Name, Image, and Likeness rights (formally called Rights of Publicity) for college athletes with the initial effective date of January 1, 2023.

> **I'VE NEVER DONE ANYTHING SO DEMANDING, AND YET, SO ENJOYABLE.**

When it passed, I was building a strategic plan on behalf of the American Volleyball Coaches Association to get beach volleyball added as a collegiate sport for men. I was deep in studying the economics of intercollegiate athletics, budgets, and trying to figure out how I could convince athletic departments to *add* a men's sport in an era of cutting men's sports.

Immediately after SB206 passed, the NCAA went on the defensive. They threatened lawsuits. They threatened to forbid the California schools from competing in the championships—potentially in the NCAA at all. Multiple national news outlets picked up the story, and it seemed like at that moment, everyone had their eyes on those three letters: NIL.

The topic absolutely fascinated me. What would happen if the NCAA kicked out the California schools? Would another organization pop up to take them in? Would California schools get all the best recruits because they would allow athletes to monetize their NIL? Would other schools leave the NCAA to join this new organization? I hypothesized endlessly and debated the topic with anyone who would engage. This was pivotal. This was going to change the landscape of college sports forever.

Fast forward a year to the fall of 2020 when an article popped up about NIL. I opened it, confused about how an entire year had passed since I'd last thought of those three letters. The article highlighted a few key events coming up in 2021. First, the NCAA would vote on NIL reform in early January, and then, if nothing definitive came of that meeting, Florida's own NIL bill was going into effect on July 1.

This meant, NIL was going into effect in at least one state in 2021. The moment was here.

Although the pandemic was wildly distracting, the NIL deadlines didn't change and were quickly approaching. While I wasn't paying attention, NIL had gotten onto the fast track. If this caught me off guard, as someone who was so fascinated with this topic and was completely invested just a year prior, how many other people across the country were possibly paying attention to this?

After a quick google search, it was apparent that not only was NIL reform swept under the rug by the pandemic, but there wasn't even a hub of content people could visit to understand the massive change that was coming to college sports the following year.

Could I develop that hub? Could I build a social media following? Could I share information and help people understand this rapidly developing and complex industry that was right around the corner?

Why not? Relentless pursuit.

Twenty dollars later, I was the proud owner of nilnetwork.com with zero idea of what was ahead.

The Pillars: Authenticity and Transparency

"You should stop calling NIL Network a passion project."

"Say 'we', not 'I', when referring to NIL Network."

My friend's tips may have been solid business advice, but these ideas conflicted with two of my personal core values: authenticity and transparency.

I realize calling NIL Network a "passion project" doesn't help its credibility. I understand that using "I" instead of "we" reveals that there is only an "I" behind the business.

But it *is* a passion project, and I *am* the singular person working on NIL Network.

If being too honest causes me to fail, so be it. I would rather fail with authenticity than succeed with deception. And you know what? For the most part, it's worked out just fine.

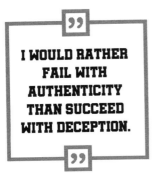

I WOULD RATHER FAIL WITH AUTHENTICITY THAN SUCCEED WITH DECEPTION.

The past year has included dozens of "firsts" that have brought excitement, nervousness, and uncomfortable situations. I've seen both ends of entrepreneurship: being taken aback by the incredible support I received from some and, unfortunately, being manipulated by someone I naively trusted.

Every step of the way has pushed me to get comfortable being uncomfortable. To accept I'm doing the best I can, staying true to my north star, and being authentic and transparent in everything I do.

The Lessons and the Experiences

My initial idea with NIL Network was to aggregate articles and write synopses. It was ugly, time-consuming, and seemingly pointless. My first month of NIL Network brought a whopping forty-seven users. I carried on. I was once again captivated by this topic and figured I might as well share with whoever stumbled across my random website.

People started reaching out on Instagram. Founders started asking to meet. "I've fooled another one!" I'd text my friends when another CEO asked for a meeting.

With each milestone and each new opportunity came a wave of emotions: uncertainty, giddiness, fear. And eventually, reflections and lessons. That's what I want to share with you here.

February 2021: First Business Meeting

I'm not sure what I expected to happen when I started moving forward with developing NIL Network. My introverted self probably hoped I could just read articles and share my thoughts without ever having to talk to anyone.

That being said, the first meeting request I got from the CEO of a prominent NIL company sent me into a panic. What did he want from me? Was I in trouble? How in the world could I fill thirty minutes?

> EVERY STEP OF THE WAY HAS PUSHED MY INTROVERTED SELF TO GET COMFORTABLE WITH BEING UNCOMFORTABLE.

I mulled over this for days leading up to our call: "There's no way he could be mad. You're doing a good service." I replayed that over and over again in my head.

Turns out, my fears were one-hundred percent unwarranted. Jason was fantastic. He was an enthusiastic entrepreneur navigating this new space. He wanted to understand the vision for NIL Network and if there were any opportunities for collaboration. He wanted to support me in my NIL goals.

And a year later, he's still one of my biggest supporters.

Takeaway: Ask for the meeting. Be willing to take meetings. In the past year, I've met with hundreds of people in and around the NIL industry. Have they all been fruitful? Absolutely not.However, I'm always pleasantly surprised by the continuing camaraderie, support, and partnerships that have come from some of those meetings.

As a solo entrepreneur, a few of these people have essentially become my coworkers. They are there to talk about trends, share insights, and navigate this new industry.

April 2021: First Podcast Recording

When Taylor, a man from New Zealand who resembles a lost Hemsworth brother, asked me to be on his podcast to discuss NIL, I was terrified. It was one thing to meet one-on-one; it was a whole different landscape to record and broadcast my opinions to whoever cared to tune in. However, because of my inability to say 'no' to a cute face and a kiwi accent, I agreed.

While I was absolutely terrified beforehand, stumbling through-out, and over-thinking every word I said, I did it. And I survived. I'm not sure I've ever listened to that recording, nor will I, but it was an important step in finding my voice and developing confidence.

It took me a while to understand that there are varying levels of podcasting. The one Tay invited me to do, pre-recorded, was not that intimidating. You have a conversation, and you get to remove any piece you don't like. You can even re-record seg-ments that didn't come out right, and you get to put your best foot forward.

This has been the setup for almost all the podcasts I've been invited onto, and ninety-nine percent of the time, I don't have any change requests. Because of this soft introduction to podcasting, I've found the confidence to do recordings with a live audience—some-thing I *never* would've considered just a year ago.

Takeaways: Establishing my voice has been one of my biggest challenges. Sharing my opinions, being vulnerable, and open-ing myself up to criticism is the worst nightmare for an introvert like myself. However, it is so important to build credibility and trust within the community. Once I understood that the pre-re-corded version of podcasting wasn't too threatening, I went all in.

Tay and I ran a weekly NIL podcast for a few months, and since then, I've never turned down an opportunity to come on and speak.

June 2021: First Speaking Engagement

With my background in volleyball, I've had a great relationship with the executive director of the American Volleyball Coaches Association for the past decade. When I was starting NIL Network, she was one of the first people I asked to get feedback. Kathy DeBoer is an incredible leader and role model. She is full of ideas, always open to a conversation, and constantly looks for ways to empower the next generation.

At one of our early meetings, she asked if I'd be interested in speaking at the next D1 Head Coaches Meeting about NIL. Once again, my internal voice was saying, "Absolutely not. You're not prepared; you don't know anything about NIL. They will find out you are a *fraud*." Once again, I needed to be comfortable, being uncomfortable.

ESTABLISHING MY VOICE HAS BEEN ONE OF MY BIGGEST CHALLENGES.

Leading up to that webinar may have been my worst case of imposter syndrome ever. I had never done an external presentation before. I didn't believe I knew more about NIL than these D1 coaches.

During the presentation, I felt even more like an imposter. I stumbled over my words. Nobody asked questions. I was visibly nervous. I felt like a complete failure.

Kathy, being the wonderful human that she is, offered words of encouragement via text after, "Good job! Very helpful overview.

I don't know if they can think about anything but recruiting right now, but hopefully."

Takeaways: Doing something for the first time doesn't have to be, and it most likely won't be, perfect. Or even close to it. But that's okay. Growth comes from a series of mini failures. Reflecting on those failures, identifying areas for improvement, and trying again is how we get better.

Since that minor failure, I've taken part in another dozen or so speaking engagements. I'm still not happy with my delivery, but I'm happy with the continued growth, lessons, and progression after completing each one.

July 2021: First National Media Interview

In the first week of July, as everyone was waking up to the decision by the NCAA to allow college athletes to make money, the first negative story broke: One company signed thousands of college athletes to a NIL deal. The problem? Their contract granted rights to the company well beyond the compensation for the athletes they signed.

The "contract" was hidden behind a "check here to agree to the terms" checkbox. It's almost certain that no athletes read that contract, and now, they gave away the rights to their NIL in perpetuity.

An attorney in Florida brought the injustice to light, and I re-shared it on the NIL Network Instagram account. The post went viral and attracted the attention of some national media outlets. Before I knew it, I had given an interview to a reporter. She quickly published an article where my comments were squished between two leading NIL sports attorneys.

Takeaway: Media interview requests are a landscape I've never navigated in my professional career prior to this. I continue to learn and adapt my approach with each interview, but the one lesson that stands out from this first interview request is this: Don't be afraid to ask questions. "When are you aiming to publish this article?", "Who else is contributing?", "Can you give backlinks to my website?", etc.

While they may not give all the answers or fulfill requests, making the conversation two-sided and gathering information makes the process smoother and less intimidating.

September 2021: First Appearance on a Sports Network

I was very surprised to open my email one September morning and find a request to appear on a Midwest sports network. When the surprise subsided, that familiar feeling of excitement and uneasiness set in.

I knew this was a fantastic opportunity, and I had to say "yes", but this was another first that would push me outside of my ever-expanding comfort zone. The show was hosted by a former MLB player and they were bringing in an established sports agent. The imposter syndrome was overwhelming.

Just like my previous experiences, every-thing exceeded my expectations, and the host was fantastic. He directed questions to me that were NIL network-specific and ques-

> **DON'T BE AFRAID TO ASK QUESTIONS.**

tions to the sports agent that were in his wheelhouse. Although I wish my nerves didn't show through on video quite as much, overall, it was a success.

Takeaways: Something I've struggled with as an introvert is constantly questioning the value I can provide. Why are they asking me to do this? What could I possibly know that they didn't?

I think there's a healthy balance between knowing you don't know it all and understanding that you bring insights within your niche. From this experience, I try to speak with confidence on the aspects of NIL I know well and be okay with saying "I don't know" if I'm not familiar with the topic.

June — October 2021: Managing My First Interns

One of the biggest learning curves I experienced in the first year of launching NIL Network was managing interns. I had two amazing young women who were studying sports law and were ready to contribute to NIL Network projects. The problem? I was a *terrible*, and I mean, terrible, manager for them. I had a hard time delegating tasks, was constantly pivoting, and left them wondering if there was actual value in doing what I asked of them.

Furthermore, I didn't outline projects beforehand and have my teammates agree to the work and time required. I always felt hesitant asking them to do tedious tasks. As a result, both sides were constantly frustrated, and I made the tough decision to end the internships earlier than expected.

Takeaways: After ending the internships, I did some introspection about my management style and how I could make the experience better for future interns. I learned that with my management style, the more I could develop a project scope and communicate expectations prior to interns beginning work for NIL Network, the more smoothly things would go.

Four months after I ended the previous internship, I took on another intern. This time, it is going much better. This young man knows the timeline, deliverables, and expectations. We meet once a week to go over progress from the past week and make a plan for the next. I feel confident with my new approach and think I'll have success with many interns going forward.

November 2021 — January 2022: Presenting at My First Conferences

Over the summer and fall, I did NIL webinars for the memberships of six different coaching associations. I was elated when four of them asked me to speak in person at their upcoming conferences. More so than the opportunity to attend conferences in different sports and build the brand of NIL Network, that they asked me to present *again* meant I couldn't possibly be as terrible as I thought I was.

Presenting in person is *different*. It gives you the opportunity to connect directly with people in the audience, get a pulse of the crowd, and unfortunately, be very cognizant of all the empty seats. My four sessions were sparsely attended. I tried not to take it personally—this is a new industry, and many coaches were not quite ready to embrace it.

I made sure to always thank and praise the coaches who did attend: "*You* are the early adopters that can take advantage of NIL as a recruiting advantage."

Takeaways: Every conference provided learning opportunities.

Conference One: Stick around after you're finished presenting to answer questions from those who aren't confident enough to ask them in front of the group.

This one should've been obvious for an introvert like myself who would never ask a question in front of a group.

However, I had never thought about what to do when I finished presenting. I bolted so quickly from the room people did not even have time to look up from their laptops.

Conference Two: Always have access to a clock or timer to pace yourself.

I'm not sure how it happened, but when I eventually found a clock during this presentation, I was seventy-five percent through my slides and only twenty minutes into an hour-long presentation. Panic set in.

How in the world would I talk for an additional thirty minutes with just a few slides left? A small miracle happened when the microphone went out, and I was able to pause for five minutes while the tech crew worked on the issue. Unfortunately, the issue wasn't solved, and I ended up having to finish sans microphone and only ten minutes early.

> **MOST NEGATIVITY HAS EVERYTHING TO DO WITH THE PERSON PROJECTING IT AND LITTLE TO DO WITH YOURSELF.**

Conference Three: Don't take things personally. Most negativity has everything to do with the person projecting it and little to do with yourself.

At this conference, my learnings happened during one of the hosted networking events. I was chatting with a few coaches, and another walked over.

When I told her I worked in the NIL space, her whole demeanor changed. She began ranting about NIL being the worst thing to happen to college sports, how it makes her want to retire from coaching, and how she can't believe people are actually in support of it. I felt attacked, got upset, and let this coach ruin my evening.

Conference Four: Check the weather before you go.

This one probably seems silly to most, but it was something I needed to be reminded of. While I spent little time outside because I didn't have the appropriate clothes, the short time that I did was miserable. This southern California girl was not prepared for Kansas City in January.

February 2022: First Time Co-Authoring a Book

Finally, and most recently, is the opportunity to co-author a book. Full transparency, I've co-authored a book before—kind of. When I was twelve years old, I won an essay contest in American Girl magazine to share my experience as a young athlete. A dozen young girls from around the United States and myself were published in a book titled, "Throw Like a Girl".

I remember how excited I was to attend book signings in northern California and sit next to the actual authors of the book while they read excerpts and talked about their vision for the book.

This time around, sharing my story has been a challenging yet rewarding experience. It made me reflect on the past year, realize the personal growth and milestones I've been through, and give myself a little credit for what I've been able to accomplish.

Final Takeaways for Finding Your Voice

Build Your Network: Try to say "yes" to every opportunity you can. You never know what door a random meeting request will open for you.

Trust Your Instincts: Your gut feeling is your north star meeting your values. If you want to go against your instincts, really dive into your "why".

Get Very Comfortable Being Uncomfortable: Until I sat down to write this story, I actually hadn't reflected on how often I was incredibly uncomfortable over the last year. However, I survived and continued pushing into unfamiliar terrain.

Don't be Afraid to Ask for Help: It is incredible how willing people are to help, collaborate, and listen. If you think someone can help you, reach out.

Find Joy in the Puzzle of Entrepreneurship: Throughout this process, I've thought about throwing my laptop against the wall multiple times. However, my overall experience of diving into the website analytics, figuring out what works on the Instagram account, and strategizing around all aspects of building NIL Network has been one of the most fulfilling experiences of my life. I know that longevity is there because I genuinely enjoy the process I've created for myself.

ABOUT MICHELLE

Michelle Meyer is a former collegiate and professional athlete and has coached volleyball at multiple Division 1 universities. She began extensively researching Name, Image, and Likeness (NIL) reform in 2019 when California passed a bill permitting college athletes in California to monetize their NIL. A year later, she founded NIL Network to bring awareness and clarity to this massive change in collegiate sports.

In under a year, she established herself as a national thought leader in the NIL space, consulting with over one-hundred NIL companies, executives of varying associations, and dozens of athletic directors, coaches, and athletes.

CHAPTER EIGHT

ATHLETES TO ATHLETES

By Reid Meyer

My journey to becoming a six-figure athlete is best told through a story. It may seem a bit like a biography at first, but I promise there is a method to my madness!

I wasn't the greatest student in high school. In fact, I was sent to a private school in my hometown because my parents were nervous I'd do the bare minimum to pass my classes at the local public high school. The worst part of that whole situation? They were absolutely right. I was much more interested in playing sports throughout my high school career, and I would famously forget to do my homework on the days it might conflict with any athletic commitment.

Growing up, I played as many sports as I could growing up. As I got older, it became clear I had a particular talent for baseball. I was tall, left-handed, and incredibly scared of contact sports. I got to practice my pitching in the fall when everyone else in Texas was playing football. I made the varsity roster my freshman year. By the time I was a sophomore in high school, I was already getting recruitment letters from colleges around the country.

The rest of my high school baseball career continued to trend upward as I broke school records, won every award offered in my school's conference, and continued to get college attention both through my high school and club baseball team. My name was synonymous with baseball at my school, and my weekends filled up with invitational camps and college visits.

Ultimately, I ended up signing my National Letter of Intent with Texas Tech University, accepting a generous athletic scholarship at a Power 5 Big XII program. It was an opportunity that most high school baseball players only dream about. And there I was, living that dream.

End of story, right? I'm awesome. I got a baseball scholarship. Now, my life is complete! That would be great and so much easier, but that's not where this story ends.

In fact, by the end of my college career, I would attend four schools in three and a half years, quit baseball halfway through, and receive a diagnosis of both depression and body dysmorphia after just one semester in college. So, let's revisit my high school timeline to see how I got there.

When I started getting attention for my ability on the baseball field, my environment shifted. My identity morphed from just Reid Meyer to Reid Meyer, the baseball player. My athletic achievements dominated more and more of the conversation around me. By the time I started getting college letters sophomore year, my identity became fully defined by what I contributed to my sport.

In a way, it was incredibly exciting. I had discovered this thing I was good at. Everyone wants to have a talent, and mine just so happened to be for a sport my community cared about. The more success I had, the more attention I got. Whether it was coaches, peers, parents, or the overall community, it was an incredibly powerful motivator for a fourteen-year-old boy.

> **WHEN I STARTED GETTING ATTENTION FOR MY ABILITY ON THE BASEBALL FIELD, MY ENVIRONMENT SHIFTED.**

The validation I got from baseball was like a drug, and it quickly became a top priority in my life. As my personal investment in the sport grew, so did the investment of the people who supported me.

My parents knew I wanted to play baseball at the next level, so they began paying for lessons and signing me up for more competitive and financially demanding teams. They did everything they could think of to put me in a position to succeed. Not a day goes by that I don't appreciate their support, but it created an expectation that I needed to provide a payoff for the investment my parents were making in me.

For those of you who'd like to check the scoreboard, I am a white man attending a private high school in Texas with parents who are willing and able to financially invest in my sport aspirations. If this had been a video game, one could argue I started my journey on the easiest possible setting.

With that background in mind, let's continue to revisit my high school experience. I went to a private school in my hometown and never took advantage of the resources available to me because they had nothing to do with sports. I was much more interested in playing baseball throughout my high school career. Frequently, I prioritized my athletics over my academics because I convinced myself that my value would be measured on the baseball field, not in a classroom.

I missed volleyball tournaments with my friends because there were baseball practices on the weekends. I didn't play basketball because I could injure myself before baseball season. As I mentioned, I made the varsity roster my freshman year but barely cracked a smile because anything less would have felt like a failure.

When I was a sophomore in high school, I got my first, personalized recruiting letter from Virginia Tech University. Then I spent the next few months mailing out dozens of personalized packets to higher-ranked Division I schools. I viewed the letter as a baseline, not an achievement.

Baseball dominated the rest of my high school career. I missed friends' birthday parties, skipped meetings with my high school's college counselors, and traveled to what felt like every showcase camp within a 500-mile radius of my house. I felt my only unique identifier amongst my peers was baseball, and I put my interests outside of the sport in a mental box. Out of sight.

In August of my senior year, my plan to attend an Ivy League school blew up in my face when Dartmouth University could no longer honor my verbal commitment. I didn't prioritize my academics enough in high school, so they could not recommend me to the admissions office. I assumed my athletic ability would supersede the need for great grades, but I was wrong.

Struggling with rejection, I committed to Weatherford Junior College because it was close to home, and the coach I had been working with for years was now their pitching coach. However, I still attended several showcase camps in the fall of senior year in a desperate attempt to catch the attention of another Division I program.

After a strong showing in an Arizona camp, I signed with Texas Tech University on the very last day of the early signing period, roughly three days after my official visit, despite not enjoying my time in Lubbock. They were offering a generous athletic scholarship at a Big XII program. It was an opportunity that most high school baseball players only dream about, so I felt pressured accept.

To this day, I still remember sitting in the coach's office at Weatherford Junior College with tears in my eyes, telling my coach I had to retract my commitment to Weatherford because I was going to sign with Texas Tech.

Everyone in that room knew I didn't want to go to Texas Tech. For the last four years, I had attached my value to my athletic achievements. NCAA Division I baseball was considered the pinnacle of college athletics. If I had an opportunity to reach the top, why wouldn't I take it?

Same timeline, different perspectives. If you only focus on athletics, I navigated high school very well. However, once you start to broaden the scope and look at my overall experience, it paints a completely different picture.

Fast forward to the start of my freshman year in college. My mother dropped me off in Lubbock, Texas, and I didn't even know what my college major was. I was assigned something over the summer during orientation, but the only thing that seemed to matter was whether or not it would conflict with baseball practice.

We called this "majoring in eligibility". I later found out I was an exercise science major, specifically in a program designed

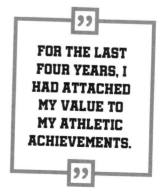

FOR THE LAST FOUR YEARS, I HAD ATTACHED MY VALUE TO MY ATHLETIC ACHIEVEMENTS.

to send kids to physical therapy school. It was not the most logical major for someone who passes out when they see injuries.

Fall training began the day before classes started, and my undergraduate career felt like a whirlwind from day one. Coming from a small school in Texas, I was always "the guy" on any team I played for. When I got to Texas Tech, I became "just some guy" instead.

As someone who valued themselves based on athletics, this was hard to handle. Mentally, I felt like I was underperforming because I wasn't the top athlete for every drill. My response was to put more time into my sport so I could compete with the rest of my team.

While competition is traditionally healthy, I created an unhealthy balance for myself. By the time I went home for winter break, I had lost roughly sixty pounds in four months. I entered Texas Tech at 6'4", 195 pounds, so I did not have sixty pounds to lose.

My sister pulled me aside when I visited home and basically forced me to dial a psychiatrist before leaving her sight. After some sessions over winter break, the therapist diagnosed me with depression and body dysmorphia. They put me on an antidepressant called Lexapro.

During the spring season, I finally realized that the athletic side of my college experience was not satisfying. I was constantly disappointed in myself for my performance. I was constantly anxious about practice, games, and everything in between. I didn't feel like my existence was contributing to the team After two cumulative innings in four appearances over the course of my freshman season, I called my mother on the way home from Lubbock and told her I was transferring schools.

I didn't want to lose a year of eligibility. However, I felt like I needed to go somewhere familiar in order to get some of my mojo back. And that's what I did. I ended up walking on at Weatherford Junior College my sophomore year. In my mind, this was a stepping-stone to getting back into the Division I cycle, but it ended up being the last resting place of my competitive baseball career.

The fall season, which happens at the junior college level, was incredibly successful for me. I was easily one of the top pitchers on the team. It felt like I had true value again for the first time since my senior year of high school. I was riding high, taking official visits to different colleges again. By the time we got to winter break, I had multiple competitive scholarship offers from several Division I schools.

In an effort to avoid another Texas Tech situation, I approached my visits differently this time. Instead of focusing on just athletics, I would listen to my gut more than usual as I toured the campus, spoke with coaches, and met other players on the team.

However, as I toured colleges and spoke with coaches, I realized I cared less and less about the baseball part of the trip. Topics that used to occupy the entirety of my brain in high school were struggling to keep my attention.

I found myself much more interested in the campus, the classrooms, and opportunities outside of baseball. I didn't know it at the time, but Texas Tech had pulled the curtain back on college athletics. I didn't value that part of my college experience the same way I used to.

I decided to delay my commitment until the spring semester, and that would prove to be one of the smarter decisions of my college career. Weatherford struggled early in the season. After a few tough weekends, our head coach met with players individually. He wanted to know where our priorities were in the spring, and he seemed convinced we had to choose between school and sport.

Under normal circumstances, I would have said "sport" whether I believed it or not, because we all know what a coach wants to hear. I didn't do that. I told him I loved baseball, but I would not be a professional player, so I needed to focus on my academics just as much as I did the baseball season. After that meeting, I didn't pitch another inning until our sophomore night. I went from being one of the most highly recruited players in the fall to sitting the entire season out. That was the last sign I needed to see.

Halfway through the spring season, I contacted every coach who offered me a scholarship, and I told them all the same thing—I'm done playing college baseball. Some were confused, some didn't care, and some thought I was lying.

At first, that decision haunted me. I felt like I had wasted everyone's time with my college baseball career. For a while, I even contemplated killing myself because I couldn't see my personal value beyond sports. It felt easier to end things on my own terms instead of having to admit to everyone I didn't live up to my athletic expectations. It may seem extreme, but I'm far from the only athlete who has struggled with these thoughts.

I expected to feel a pain in my chest after the last phone call since I effectively ended my own baseball career, but I just felt relief. I knew I would miss playing my sport on a competitive level, but my relationship with baseball had become so toxic over the last two years I knew stepping away was the right decision.

Telling my parents was tougher. I'm convinced they thought I was joking at first. They were convinced it was just a fleeting feeling that would pass over the course of a few days. I had to tell them it had been on my mind for the past several months, and the amount of relief I felt after those phone calls only validated my emotions.

I remember the major source of my fear when I talked to my parents. It stemmed from the idea that they would be disappointed in me. I could already hear them reminding me how much they spent over the course of my childhood and the number of weekends they sacrificed for me to play a tournament in the middle of nowhere. It felt unfair to me, and I was willing to take that anger after my decision.

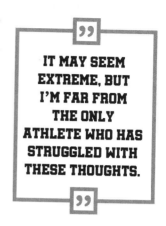

IT MAY SEEM EXTREME, BUT I'M FAR FROM THE ONLY ATHLETE WHO HAS STRUGGLED WITH THESE THOUGHTS.

My parents didn't mention it once in our entire conversation. They wanted to know that the decision I was making was with a clear mind, and they wanted to know that the decision made me happy. That was it. I know that not every family would respond the same way, but I'm eternally grateful my parents supported me through that decision.

Now it was time to pick a school without the influence of athletics. Baseball had always been my crutch, and so far, it had sent me to two different schools in less than two years. I visited colleges to see friends this time, not coaches. Ultimately, I attended the University of Texas. I had to take a few classes at Austin Community College to graduate on time, which is how I got to my fourth college in under four years.

My first semester at UT had to be the most transformative during the duration of my entire college career. For the first time since early high school, I was no longer Reid, the baseball player, and I had forgotten how to be just Reid.

Athlete re-identification is a genuine struggle, no matter when it hits you. Trying to re-establish who I was while adjusting to a new environment in Austin was something I was not at all prepared for. It took time, therapy, and a lot of trial and error before I felt like I was standing on solid ground again.

While I may have stepped away from baseball, many of my tendencies are still connected to sports. As I was completing my final semester of college, I found it impossible not to reflect on my college experience as a whole.

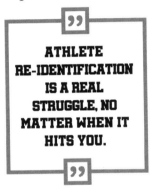

ATHLETE RE-IDENTIFICATION IS A REAL STRUGGLE, NO MATTER WHEN IT HITS YOU.

At first, there was a lot of frustration in that process because I would look back and sulk about how disjointed my college experience was. All my full-time student friends had a great college experience, building relationships that would continue after college. They had a clear idea of what their next steps were going to be after college. As I sat in my one-bedroom apartment filling out applications for baseball facilities in my hometown so I could live at home and avoid paying rent, I couldn't help but feel cheated out of the true college experience.

The more I thought about it, the more I saw my situation as a puzzle to solve. Where did it go wrong? Were there warnings I missed? How could I have improved my college experience? I started writing questions on notecards and pinning the notes to my wall.

After a few days, I had filled the entire kitchen wall with notecards and accepted that I was probably not getting my security deposit back. I went through each card one by one, and for each question, I would do my best to answer it as objectively as possible, given my own experiences.

This process was better than any medicine I was ever prescribed. At first, I only answered the questions based on my own experiences. Soon after, I started researching the topics to see if I could add some empirical evidence to my resolutions.

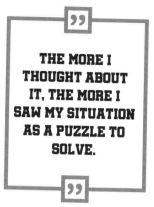

THE MORE I THOUGHT ABOUT IT, THE MORE I SAW MY SITUATION AS A PUZZLE TO SOLVE.

Finally, I began reaching out to my other student-athlete friends. Despite my effort to network as a full-time student, the vast majority of my friends were still student-athletes actively competing in college athletics.I was amazed and sometimes relieved to find that for every question I asked myself, there were at least two other people I knew who had asked themselves the very same question.

In fact, I added to my wall of questions after talking to each of my friends because they had questions I hadn't thought of initially.

All in all, I discovered my story was far from the exception and—in fact—was much closer to the rule. While no athlete's experience is the same, there are certainly common themes that affect all college athletes. I realized that most of these problems could be mitigated or managed in a healthy way by educating and empowering student-athletes at the high school level about common issues and pitfalls we're well-aware of within that student demographic.

What started as notecards on a kitchen wall eventually grew into my company, Athletes to Athletes. The business wasn't profitable right away, nor was it even a real business, but I knew I had unlocked a purpose in my life that wouldn't go away.

My passion is helping athletes navigate the college selection process with far more support than I ever had.. I knew there was a way to do it through education and mentorship. You're probably

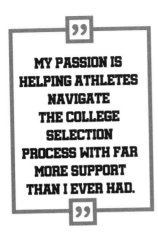

MY PASSION IS HELPING ATHLETES NAVIGATE THE COLLEGE SELECTION PROCESS WITH FAR MORE SUPPORT THAN I EVER HAD.

wondering what the point of this chapter may be. Simply put, I wanted to showcase an example where passion and chance create opportunity.

My college experience didn't go the way I planned. In fact, it went about as far from the plan as humanly possible. If you look at my experience in a vacuum, many would claim it was more failure than success, and I can't entirely disagree with them. The culmination of my experience created an opportunity for me to discover a passion.

Most would consider my early exit from baseball an unfortunate result. I've come to see it as one of the luckiest moments of my life because it freed me from choosing the next school based entirely on athletics. It also opened my eyes to the opportunity to help the next generation of student-athletes avoid the same mistakes I made.

Life experiences, both good and bad, can be your most powerful asset when creating a business. I would strongly encourage you to view them as opportunities rather than obstacles.

ABOUT REID

Reid Meyer is the co-founder and CEO of Athletes to Athletes, a college counseling company for high school student-athletes. As a standout pitcher in high school, Reid attended Texas Tech University as a member of the baseball team.

After a tumultuous playing career in college, he ultimately earned his undergraduate degree and master's degree from the University of Texas. Before launching his own business, he worked for a sports streaming startup, FloSports.

Reid has a passion for helping student-athletes, and his company aims to help that population make holistic college decisions that satisfy them academically, athletically, personally, and financially. Reid is a member of TACAC, NACAC, NCAG, IECA, and a graduate of the Independent Educational Consulting program at UC Irvine.

CHAPTER NINE

FROM BASKETBALL HOOPS TO BUSINESS SUITS

By Alex Opacic

A s soon as I stepped onto the basketball court at age twelve, I fell in love. I admit, football was my first love, but it did not compare to basketball. My natural footwork, ability, and the hand-eye coordination I developed from playing football from age three enabled me to dominate the sport instantly. My height at 6'9" only added to my skills.

Basketball became my passion. I gained a deep desire to keep playing, winning, and continuously getting better. The same year I started playing, I watched this *Michael Jordan* guy play. I wanted to be just like Mike—c'mon, if any pro-baller out there says they didn't wanna be just like Mike, they're lying! I began having this deep obsession for the game—dribbling the ball to and from school, and I played before, during, and after school. There were many nights

I fell asleep with the ball in my bed. It's all I ever spoke about and all I ever wanted to do!

I had a dream of playing college basketball and becoming a pro-basketball player. It was like the NBA was calling my name before I graduated high school.

Given this love and obsession for the game, I started emerging as one of the best players in the country for my age. Toward the end of high school, all my hard work started paying off as I was awarded a scholarship at the Australian Institute of Sport (AIS). I was afforded the opportunity to play alongside some of today's NBA stars and greatest Aussie sports heroes—Patty Mills, Joe Ingles, and Aaron Baynes, to name a few.

The AIS not only gave me a chance to make my dreams a reality, but more importantly, it taught me the meaning of hard work and how to fight for what you want. Studying and playing basketball overseas gave me the opportunity to work and collaborate with multiple personalities from various cultural backgrounds. It taught me the art of building relationships with different people by adjusting my style to fit the personality type.

My days consisted of five-plus hours of training, studying, physiotherapy work, and learning about nutrition—health, body, and mind. Training taught me that suffering is good—even if I didn't learn it right away.

Discipline became a habit. I adopted a strong work ethic and learned how to implement time management with my schedule. Not only did my time at AIS create resiliency, but it also taught me how to compete, the importance of team-work, and so much more. I still implement these lessons to this day.

The passion, desire, and hard work led me to a full basketball scholarship at Furman University, a NCAA Division 1 school in South Carolina. Another dream come true!

DISCIPLINE BECAME A HABIT.

During those four years, I competed against some of the best 18 to 23-year-olds in the world, including Steph Curry (I had to throw that in there). I met some amazing people from all over the world and graduated with a degree in communication.

My nickname in college was "Big Friendly Giant". Our campus had various groups that stuck with each other: athletes, international students, science nerds, law students, and chess club members. I tried to be involved with all of them. I loved meeting new people. Their stories fascinated me and I showed genuine interest in everyone I met. In return, most people, no matter what group they felt like, loved being around me, too.

The biggest lesson I learned at university was how to be emotionally intelligent. I wasn't aware of this at the time. In fact, I didn't figure it out until years later, but I'm extremely grateful because of it.

All my energy, passion, and focus remained on basketball. Upon graduating with a 2.0 GPA and having the time of my life in college, I earned a professional contract in Europe. I was able to play in Greece, Cyprus, Macedonia, and Croatia. Another dream come true! I felt on top of the world. Not only was I playing professional basketball across Europe, but I was also able to see some amazing places, visit the most beautiful beaches, and meet some incredible people.

Whilst in Macedonia, I was an all-star, and my team made the championship game. Even though we lost in the final, I felt extremely proud of what we achieved as a team, and equally as important, I felt invincible as I was being successful as a professional basketball player.

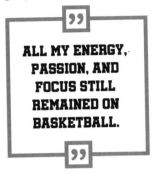

ALL MY ENERGY, PASSION, AND FOCUS STILL REMAINED ON BASKETBALL.

Two years into my pro-career, I developed an overuse knee injury. I was never good at resting and taking extended time away from the game. Even in the off-season, I was always working on my game. This caused my knee to break down over time, and during my second year of playing professionally, my meniscus tore.

When the doctor delivered the news and explained I would need surgery, it was like he took one-hundred bricks and threw them in my face. One minute I was on top of the world, the next I was in the gutter. I had that horrible sick feeling in my stomach, coupled with a stab to the heart. It genuinely felt like the love of my life was breaking up with me, leaving me to rot.

I ended up having two surgeries and was forced to sit out for at least one-and-a-half years. When I returned home to Sydney, I had no choice but to find a job. I was lost! I had zero skills and no confidence in anything outside of basketball. I didn't know who to turn to for help or how to even go about finding a job.

At age twenty-four, I felt completely useless, worthless, and sad. My self-esteem was at an all-time low, and I had no hope for any kind of future. I locked myself in my room, and at times, refused to talk to anyone—even my parents. I was too ashamed to be in front of them as a failure. So, I laid on the couch, neglected most of my friends, ate a lot of junk food, put on weight, refused to watch basketball, and avoided being seen in public. This lasted the whole year and half of my knee rehabilitation.

I became accustomed to waking up every day chasing a dream and following a passion which became more like an obsession, so I didn't know what to do with myself when my knee injury killed my dream. I had no other passion or dream to chase, and it felt empty and hard to accept and to move on.

Most of my life, I had a one-track mind, and that was to become a professional basketball player. Not once did it cross my mind that basketball would not last forever. I wish I would have thought about reading books, learning about other things, and finding another passion. I thought I was going to play until I was in my seventies.

Looking back on this experience, I learned the lesson of never putting all my eggs in one basket and to search for another passion whilst you're still a pro-athlete.

After my knee somewhat recovered, I was good enough for a semi-pro contract in Albury-Wodonga, and it was the start of the best thing that happened to me (career-wise). To supplement my basketball contract, I needed to get a full-time job as well.

I met a media sales manager who saw the potential in me and offered me a job as a sales representative for one of the biggest media companies in Asia Pacific (their Albury branch). Later on, she told me that because I was an elite athlete; she knew I had the fire, resilience, and work ethic in me to be a successful sales rep. She knew I didn't know that, but she was confident enough to get it out of me.

And boy, was she right! I accepted the fact I would no longer be a pro-baller travelling across Europe. Instead, I started obsessing about my newfound career–sales! I began overachieving my targets and soon became one of the highest performers.

I read books, asked for extra training, watched YouTube tutorials, and studied my senior colleagues. I saw more success. As I mentioned previously, emotional intelligence came naturally to me. I believe I gained it from traveling the world and playing basketball. Wherever it came from, I used it to my advantage. It enabled me to forge business relationships and reach my sales targets.

The year I began my new job, my semi-pro basketball career took off. We ended up winning the national championship!

The harder I worked in media sales, the more successful I became. I used the same philosophy as sport. That basketball team I was a part of was the hardest-working, most close-knit, and dedicated team I ever played on. That's why we won! I was clever enough to apply those same principles in the business world. Three years later, it all paid off when I received a promotion into the Sydney office and moved back home.

Although I was establishing my business career, moving back to Sydney meant that my semi-pro basketball career was over. My sales career became far more demanding, and Sydney had no semi-pro basketball teams.

My basketball career was now over forever. Then it hit me! What's my dream now? As my basketball dream ended, it felt empty to have no other dream to aspire to.

What am I passionate about? Basketball was my only passion, and it felt extremely unfulfilling to do something I'm not passionate about. What am I working towards? It felt weird to not have a goal or a long-term plan/dream. I had no fulfillment in my life anymore; how would I find it again?

I somehow had faith my next passion would find me. Like with basketball, I began obsessing about becoming a successful business professional. I truly believed that, as long as I kept trying to be the best salesperson I could be, even though I wasn't passionate about my current job, my purpose would be revealed.

I listened to business podcasts such as The Tim Ferriss Show and School of Greatness by Lewis Howes. I read books such as *How to Win Friends and Influence People* and *Never Split The Difference*. I took public speaking and presentation courses, sales training, and more. In the next three years, I became infatuated with entrepreneurship.

I still wasn't passionate about my job as I didn't care about the product I was selling (radio advertising). I wanted to do bigger and better things, and I wasn't one-hundred percent happy. Unfortunately, I was one of those people who tied my happiness to my career. Today, I understand happiness and career are two separate things which I believe helps me be a better business professional and person. By listening to all those podcasts, reading business books, and trying to perfect my sales process, I somehow sensed my passion around the corner.

Along my business journey, I met a lot of former athletes who were successful in business by learning to apply the skills and attributes gained from their sport. Like myself, I also met a lot of athletes who needed help in applying the skills and attributes from sport into the business world.

That's when I had a light bulb moment. I knew businesses can benefit from having athletes on their teams, and I knew I could help other athletes transition better than I did by helping them apply the skills from their sport into the business world. My passion was born! Athlete2Business is a recruitment agency that places former pro-athletes into roles which maximize their unique skills and experiences.

As I perform the day-to-day duties at Athlete2Business, I feel like I'm playing basketball again! I'm finally fulfilled and passionate about what I do again!

I'm also lucky enough to have personal fulfillment as a husband and a father of two beautiful daughters. I also added professional fulfillment as I began chasing my new dream of becoming the global leader in athlete transition services.

I wouldn't have found this passion If I didn't:

- Work my ass off in sales and try to be the very best, even though I wasn't passionate about what I was selling.
- Apply the same principles from sport to the business world.
- Accept that basketball was over and focus on learning and developing new skills.
- Obsess about learning the best sales process and business productivity.
- Listen to all those business podcasts and read business books.
- Learn to enjoy working in Business-to-Business (B2B) sales by obsessing about the best sales process and hitting sales targets.
- Network like a beast and build towards my personal post-sport brand.
- Surround myself with like-minded, ambitious, and positive people.
- Learn how to sell and market a product/service by working in B2B sales.

Mistakes I made that other athletes should avoid:

- I didn't care about anything outside of basketball.
- I never read a non-fiction book until basketball was over.
- I failed to plan for any careers outside of basketball.
- I did the bare minimum to upskill myself while I was playing basketball.
- I wish I took university more seriously.

- I wish I hadn't taken one-and-a-half years to start applying the lessons/skills from sport into business.
- During my playing career, I should've built my post-sport network via networking events and LinkedIn.

A couple of important things I've learned are to never stop dreaming, finding passion, and aspiring for greatness. For a period of time, I lost that ambition, but once I found it again, I realized you never really stop being an athlete.

Instead of being competitive, hardworking, resilient, determined, motivated, disciplined, and focused on the court, I now apply those high-performing habits in the boardroom.

As an athlete, I was determined and driven to succeed, and of course, make a six-figure salary. However, I never did. The pursuit of this success instilled elite, high-performing habits in me, which enabled me to make six figures working in sales and high six figures as an entrepreneur.

Here's How I Did It: Working in sales is exactly the same as sport. The harder you work, the better you perform, and the more you get paid. There are targets, goals, and KPIs (Key Performance Indicators) to achieve. To earn a $120K salary as a doctor, lawyer, engineer, etc., it takes almost a decade (university, post grad, internship, entry-level, then mid-level). In sales, you can earn $120K+ in twelve months.

Let's first understand what sales is not. Sales isn't about being a smooth talker. It's not about having supreme confidence. You don't have to be an extrovert. It's not about being annoying or bothering people or being smooth with your words.

Sales is about listening and solving your customers' problems. It's about having a deep level of empathy and truly putting yourself

SALES IS ABOUT LISTENING AND SOLVING YOUR CUSTOMERS' PROBLEMS.

in your customers' shoes. It is the art of connecting, listening, and engaging with another person. Sales is human engineering—it is solving problems through conversation. That's all there is to it. It is also about being persistent (without being annoying), resilient (being able to pick yourself up after rejection), and disciplined (sticking to a process regardless of the outcome).

Most importantly, sales teaches you how to be an entrepreneur. You learn how to make money for someone else and make all the mistakes there while earning a base salary. Then, you make money for yourself.

But, before you become an entrepreneur, here is a proven sales process that will help you be a successful entrepreneur and earn six figures:

1. Prospecting
2. The Call
3. Discovery Meeting
4. Presentation/Closing the Deal

1. Prospecting:

This is the process of searching for your ideal customer. Identify the decision-maker and contact them to get a meeting. You will need to learn about their business problems and gain an opportunity to provide your product or service as the solution and win them as a customer.

Depending on the product or service you are selling, identify one-hundred businesses you can sell to. Do your research on Google,

LinkedIn, your company's CRM, etc., and find one-hundred busi-nesses in your target market.

You need to find a genuine business reason to contact these busi-nesses. I call it a VBR (Valid Business Reason). For example, if you are selling radio advertising, look for companies with multiple loca-tions in your city that need to reach a large customer base for a sale they are doing. Your sales manager or colleagues can help you iden-tify a VBR for each of the customers you found. Do *not* call anyone if you don't have a genuine VBR; you'd be wasting your time, their time and it's just unprofessional.

On an Excel document (or something similar) for each of the companies you found, write down names of any decision-makers (you can easily find them on the company website or LinkedIn page), their phone number (again, from their website or their LinkedIn profile once you've connected), and the VBR for contacting them.

Using LinkedIn premium or sales navigator, message the deci-sion-maker and structure your message like this:

— Compliment: Give them a genuine compliment which you can find on their LinkedIn page or googling their name/business.
— Intro: Who you are and what you do.
— VBR: State the reason for your call.
— Close: Ask to jump on an introductory call or meeting to show them your value.

2. The Call:

You now have your list of prospects whom you messaged on LinkedIn to get their attention.

If they haven't gotten back to you within two to three days on LinkedIn, call them to gain a meeting. Your call needs to be short, sharp, and straight to the point. People are busy, especially high-level decision-makers, so you have roughly ten seconds to win them over.

Here's the structure of your call:

— Compliment: As soon as they answer, compliment them. Their ego will love it. A genuine compliment about their recent achievements or business success.
— Introduction: Quickly introduce yourself and your company.
— VBR: Then, hit them with your valid business reason for the call. Get straight to the point about why you're calling.
— Close: Get them to commit to a forty-five-minute meeting where you can sell your product or service properly.

Here is my call script from when I was working in radio sales; feel free to use it and make it your own:

"Hi Mr. XXX, firstly I want to say huge congrats on tripling your business revenue this year, it's a huge testament to your leadership, tenacity, and work ethic. I am inspired. (Usually they say something here, so play along accordingly. Obviously, do your research to give a legit compliment.)

"My name is Alex, and I am an account manager at KIIS 106.5, #1 radio station in Sydney. The reason for my call is I noticed you're running a promotion at 30% off on all your products next week. How would you like to advertise this to our one-million weekly listeners who are looking for what you're selling?"

Never give your price on this initial call. If they are interested or asking questions, get them to commit to a meeting where you can learn more about their business and give more insight into how your product/service can be a fit, including price. Never give out too much info on the initial call. Otherwise, there is no point for an in-person/video meeting where you will have a much better chance at building a legit relationship and closing the deal.

3. Discovery Meeting:

You've won the prospect on your call, and they are keen to meet you in person to learn more about your product/service. Remember, sales are all about solving problems.

So, in this discovery meeting, you need to find out what their problems are. Everyone has problems. The only way to uncover a problem or an opportunity where you can provide your product/service as a solution is to ask intelligent questions and listen.

I use the 70/30 rule. The customer should be talking seventy percent of the time, and you should be talking thirty precent of the time. If you fail to do this, you'll most likely lose the sale.

Once you've asked intelligent questions and uncovered a problem, give them a rundown of your service/product and how you will be able to solve their problem. Based on the information you have collated from the customer, you will put together a tailored solution to solve their problem. The solution presentation should happen within a week of this discovery meeting. Before you do that, close with them before the close.

Here's how: "Mr. Client, if I was to come back next week with a tailored solution to the problem/issue/opportunity we have discovered today, at a cost of $123 (now give them a price), would you be ready to commit to this?"

It sets expectations, and if needed, you can solve all objections right there and then.

4. Presentation/The Close:

This is the final meeting where you are to present your solution to the client and close the deal. All objections should have been covered in the discovery meeting, and all you are to do is present a compelling presentation and get their signature. This should be the easiest part, as you would have also established some trust.

If they can't decide right after the presentation, keep following up until they give you an answer.

So, there it is. Prospecting, The Call, Discovery Meeting, and The Close. If you follow these four steps for working in sales, you have the potential to be earning $120K+ per year.

The key to this whole operation is having prospects to call each week. Every Monday morning, if you don't have one-hundred prospects on your list, you'll most likely be average. As an athlete, high performer, and someone who wants to earn six figures, get that one-hundred and trust the process.

Entrepreneurship:

I followed the process above for eight years and earned $100K+ for seven of them. I learned how to sell, negotiate, and build business relationships, developing a massive network for myself. Most importantly, I started understanding how to build a business from scratch.

I started my business on the side, and after two years, I jumped into it full-time. In that first year full-time (2020), we had a global pandemic and small businesses took a hit. My business (Athlete2Business) is a recruitment agency, and in 2020, businesses were mostly firing people as opposed to hiring—so I had next-to-no chance of success. Yet, in that first year, I generated $310K in revenue (mostly profit).

Here's how:

I followed a process which I called "2-2-4":

To survive in business, you need sales. In the middle of COVID-19, sales were tough to find. Businesses who were actually hiring were few and far-between. So, I had to be tough and diligent with my time and process. With the help of my business coach, I came up with a process I followed diligently, without being emotionally attached to the results.

The process is "2-2-4". That's two hours of business development (cold calling, online networking, etc., basically following the above-sales process), two hours of candidate sourcing (looking for athletes who are/can be high-performing sales professionals), and four hours of everything else, which included social media activity, running webinars, partnering with referral partners, and administration. If I did that every day, I should survive. I followed 2-2-4, and not only did I survive, I thrived.

I stuck to this process every day without being emotionally attached to the results.

The 60/30/10 Rule:

In the start-up phase of my business in 2020, sixty-percent of the time I spent on activities will generate me revenue *now*, thirty-percent of the time I spent on activities will generate revenue three to six months from now, and ten percent of the time on activities will generate revenue one year from now. You have to be mindful and commercially aware of what will generate revenue for you today and three months from now. Cash flow is king! So, get selling.

CASH FLOW IS KING!

Business Coach/Mentor:

I was lucky enough to land a business coach who was a CEO of a global recruitment agency. He accomplished what I'm trying to achieve. His wisdom has been invaluable. We have weekly, one-hour calls and quarterly, four-hour strategy sessions.

Get a mentor/coach who has been successful in your industry. In sport, you always had a coach. Business is no different.

Through my business, I've spoken to thousands of athletes in business. Like myself, I've found that most athletes find their passion/purpose again through entrepreneurship, where they are building something of their own.

There are many paths to entrepreneurship, but I've found the most effective path to be through B2B sales. Go make money for someone else whilst you're paid a base salary with a commission that will allow you to make six figures. Once you are equipped with sales skills, a network, and business acumen, venture into business for yourself, and you'll be well on your way to high-six and seven figures.

ABOUT ALEX

Alex Opacic is the founder of Athlete2Business–a global recruitment agency specializing in placing former pro-athletes into roles which maximize their unique skills and experiences.

Alex has ten years-experience as a successful Business Development Manager across media, technology, and Human Resources.

He founded his business in 2020 during a global pandemic and grew it from $0 to $300K in twelve months.

Prior to his business career, Alex was a D1 college basketball player at Furman University. He also played professionally across Europe and Australia.

Through his business, Alex has helped hundreds of athletes transition into successful, post-sport careers. You can check out his work at www.athlete2business.com.au.

CHAPTER TEN

LEVERAGE YOUR NETWORK

By Julia Rock

There are several motivational catchphrases out there when it comes to networking. One of the first that comes to mind is, "Your network equals your net worth." I'll be honest, the first time I heard those words from a mentor of mine, I thought it was pretty cliché. Well, lame honestly. But as I got deeper into corporate America, I realized how true that statement was.

My professional career has always been in accounting and finance. First, in the financial services industry, and after graduate school, in the energy sector. I have had the opportunity to work at one of the largest publicly traded oil and gas companies in the world. Not only was that position facilitated by networking, but also my career progression at the company. I'll share an example: While at an after-work event (pre-pandemic) a couple of years ago, I started chatting up one of the senior managers in my division. Many of my colleagues were talking amongst themselves, but I wanted to take advantage of the opportunity to get to know a senior leader in a low/no pressure environment because I knew building this kind of relationship, while personally beneficial, could also open doors for future roles and connections.

I'm a naturally curious person as I spent a lot of time by myself as a child and therefore had to find ways to entertain myself or learn something new. In this conversation with the manager, my curiosity was at its peak, and I asked him a lot of questions. I learned more about his perspective on certain issues at our company surrounding investment decisions and new expansion projects that were being discussed with Wall Street analysts. I used this as an opportunity to build rapport with him and showcase my knowledge.

After that event, I kept in contact with him for the next several months. We had check-in lunches where I could share some of the analytical projects I had been working on, as well as some leadership opportunities I had created for myself. Little did I know how much of an impression I was making as I was building this relationship.

The very next year, I found out that this same senior manager spoke up on my behalf in the employee performance assessment and provided context to the other senior leaders around my technical and leadership capabilities.

His input helped shift the consideration for me to receive a higher performance rating than initially expected, which also laid the foundation for my next job role. I received a promotion and expanded my management expertise. It also came with a nice salary increase!

Talk about your network working for you when you're not in the room! Having people in your network who can enter rooms you are not in can affect your career opportunities, entrepreneurial ventures, partnerships, and brand deals—the list goes on and on.

Becoming a *Six-Figure Athlete* means you've got to have the network that can actually help you generate that kind of money. Think about any of the wealthy athletes you admire. While they may have become wealthy through their sports, a major factor in maintaining and growing their wealth has been the strength of their networks.

How do you think they learn about new investment opportunities? How do you think they are able to create profitable brands with other athletes? What about identifying the right franchises to own and help launch?

Simple, their network.

They don't have to search for answers or rely on their own knowledge, or even solely their own. The depth and diversity of their network provides them with the edge and resources to make some of these money making decisions with confidence.

So, let's start with the basics. What do you think of when you hear "networking"? When most people think of networking, they think of making cold calls and exchanging business cards at an event (or sharing contact information virtually). But that networking approach is rarely effective. Why? Because it's *transactional*. It's all about meeting people with the sole purpose of hopefully getting some reward or opportunity out of it.

Valuable networking comes from focusing on developing a relationship with the contact rather than the potential transaction (we'll discuss more about this later). Networking is about creating genuine connections, then leveraging those connections for transactions.

As an athlete, you may have never thought about having to build a strong network for your career. You already had a team of coaches, trainers, and professors who were ready and willing to help you with whatever you needed.

NETWORKING IS ABOUT CREATING GENUINE CONNECTIONS, THEN LEVERAGING THOSE CONNECTIONS FOR TRANSACTIONS.

If you've never really had to plan for your career once leaving the game, the idea of needing to have a circle of people you can reach out to help open doors for you may seem foreign or even scary. How do you even get started? Who should you even network with? Where do you find these people?

To take the overwhelm out of this process, I have seven essential strategies that will help you step up your networking game:

1. **Set your goal.** Before you can step into networking, you must first set some objectives to ensure you are spending your time wisely and engaging with the right problem. To start defining your networking goals, ask yourself some basic questions:

   - What are you trying to accomplish?
   - Do you want to successfully launch your business?
   - Do you want to secure your first career role in sports beyond being an athlete?

This is not a throwaway step in the process. In order to leverage networking to its full potential for you to achieve the career or business success you are looking, it's important to be very thoughtful about what you want to achieve and why you want to achieve it. Be as *specific* as possible.

If you want to launch a business, define what kind of business you want to launch. Think about what industry you want to be in. Determine who your target audience is.

If you want your first career role, what does that look like to you? Is it working in the front office? Do you want to leave sports altogether?

Think about the companies, brands, or teams you want to work for. What industries would you want to start your next career in?

While it seems like there are a great deal of questions here, this foundation and clarity will prove very important as you determine what individuals you want to start and continue fostering relationships with.

But do keep this in mind: While your goals are important, remember that networking is not just about getting something. You don't want to meet and connect with people for the sake of asking them for favors or for help. Most people like opportunities; however, no one likes an opportunist.

2. **Define and craft your personal brand.** To be fair, personal branding could be its own chapter in this book. But the reason I wanted to include this topic along with networking is because they go hand in hand. Having a strong personal brand will make the networking process easier and more effective.

If you're not sure what I mean by "personal brand", it's essentially the perception others have of you based on how you have presented yourself. You can build this perception through your social media presence, in-person interactions, or even things like your résumé.

Why is your personal brand important to the networking process? It's essentially what you are known for, how people see you, and what they associate you with. Take Nike, for example. It's one of the best (if not *the best*) known sports apparel and footwear brands in the world. Anywhere you see the "Swoosh", you think about sneakers, fitness, sports, etc. They have built a brand that is now easily recognizable, and more importantly, clearly defined.

People know exactly what Nike offers, and what value they provide. Their brand messaging is distinct and consistent no matter which platform you see them on. You should take a similar approach when crafting your own personal brand.

When you were playing sports, you wanted people to know your name. Whether it's that you had ups like no other player on the court, or you had the skills to be a legendary three-point shooter like Steph Curry, there was something distinct about you as an athlete and your style of play that was unique. Now off the court, people knowing your name will attract new opportunities for your career. The best part is, you will be recognized without having to do all the work because your brand does the work for you!

3. **Examine and engage with your existing network.** You may think you don't have a network of people to begin with, but that just isn't true. Within your circle of contacts, you have family members, classmates, teammates, professors, coaches, perhaps agents, and even social media connections.

It is important to reflect back on the goal you outlined in Step 1 because this will help you narrow down the relationships you need to focus on. It is impossible to nurture meaningful relationships with everyone. If your goal is to successfully launch a business in the fashion industry, you would evaluate your network for entrepreneurs, brand contacts, individuals who work in retail fashion, etc. If your goal is to shift from sports and start a new career in the tech industry, you would look to reconnect with individuals in your existing sphere who are recruiters, career coaches, current or past employees, managers, or even consultants to your desired employers.

This built-in network of potential key players will allow you to strengthen relationships as you connect with these individuals to learn more about them, their experience, and their role in the field you would like to enter. This will also help you to gain more insight on what it's like to work towards and achieve your goal.

When I made the shift to become a career coach for basketball athletes instead of corporate professionals, I was slightly nervous, given I didn't have a sports background at all. But my existing network of contacts, particularly through social media, opened unexpected doors for me. Some contacts connected directly with players I could coach, which drove immediate revenue for my business. Others already had or connected me with blogs or podcast platforms to create greater visibility for my brand, now serving athletes.

I have never met any of these individuals in person, but I have taken the time to engage virtually with them on a consistent basis and actively nurture those relationships.

You may be wondering what I mean by "engage your existing network". This means actively speak and spend time with the individuals in your network. Find opportunities to organically catch up, whether it's for coffee or lunch, a virtual 15-30-minute chat just to share updates, or even just an email check-in. Send birthday wishes and celebrate the major milestones. (I have a former boss I haven't worked with since 2013, and he still sends me a birthday email every single year.)

Pro Tip: Interact with at least two people from your existing network per week. Whether you send out a quick email or text message or call, make the effort to nurture two relationships every week.

4. **Use what you've already got.** Admit it—you probably have accounts on two or three different social media platforms. You take time to scroll your feeds and interact with your followers. To take it a step further, you're already following people you find interesting and

would like to develop a relationship with. This means you already have a built-in online network you can start tapping into!

No matter the size of your following, you still have a number of people you are directly connected to for you to create organic conversations with. So why not start naturally engaging with their content, comment, share their posts/tweets, as well as upcoming events, etc.? People typically respond when you simply engage organically, without asking for anything or pitching yourself. This is much easier than sliding into someone's DMs randomly because there's a dialogue already happening on the timeline or feed.

You don't have to make this stressful by trying to work on all platforms at the same time. If you spend the majority of your social media time on Twitter, take time to connect with people there. Join Twitter Spaces (a new feature made available to all users in 2021) where you can chat with decision-makers, managers, and peers in your desired field.

If you spend time on Instagram, you can use that platform to spark conversations. Watch the livestreams of your followers and the influential contacts you want to start speaking with. Comment on their photos/posts, and share their content on your stories. Use the time you are already spending on social media to your advantage and build your earning potential.

Pro Tip: Create a LinkedIn profile. Even if it will not be the platform you spend most of your time on—it's the one primarily used for professional networking online. There are over 800+ million members and 50+ million companies on LinkedIn.

If you are looking to secure high-value brand deals or sponsorships, the decision-maker you need to talk to is most likely on

LinkedIn. If you are ready to step into a higher paying career using the skills you've built playing sports, the hiring managers and recruiters for those kinds of roles are looking for talent through LinkedIn.

To make things even easier for you, LinkedIn has the Groups feature, which allows you to search for and join groups that are most aligned with your interests. There is a group for everything and everyone. This translates to opportunities for you to tap into pockets of people who share similar ideas or may have already achieved what you are hoping to do and can offer you advice.

I know many people find LinkedIn to be less fun than the other social media platforms, but it is one of my top two platforms because it has made networking much simpler for me. I can connect with people at all levels of various companies, from the entry-level associates all the way to the C-suite executives, just by sending a personalized invitation. I can join global conversations with major brands just by commenting on a post or sharing it on my feed. I have been able to secure clients, article features, podcast interviews, and other opportunities just from sharing my expertise and making connections on LinkedIn.

5. **Get comfortable being uncomfortable.** There is no getting around this. One of the best pieces of advice I have ever received was from a former business coach of mine. She said: "You can't get to the next level if you keep doing what got you to this level. What got you here, won't get you there." That advice has completely changed how I approach my business and my life.

If you want to reach, sustain, and even surpass a six-figure salary or business income, you must be willing to do things that will stretch you and make you uncomfortable. You won't be able to stay in your comfort zone and achieve the success you are look-ing for.

As an athlete, you had to push your limits to get stronger, faster, and perform better. You had to run more laps. You had to practice when you were tired. Now that you are looking to build your brand and your income, you must be willing to push past your limits to make the connections and secure the deals you want.

This may mean reaching out to people you have never spo-ken to before or attending events you typically wouldn't sign up for on your own. It may mean being more active online than you would usually be comfortable with. You may have to speak up more in settings where you would rather be more low-key.

> **YOU WON'T BE ABLE TO STAY IN YOUR COMFORT ZONE AND ACHIEVE THE SUCCESS YOU ARE LOOKING FOR.**

But whatever the action is, know that growth comes from discomfort. Change comes from discomfort. Building a profit-able business or securing a lucrative career requires discomfort. If becoming wealthy was easy and comfortable, everyone would do it.

6. **Be willing to give, not just receive.** To build a sustainable, trust-worthy network, it can't just all be about you. If it comes across as you are only around because you are hoping to get something, you may find that the relationships end or your calls don't get returned as often. No one wants to be the only person giving in a relationship. You wouldn't like to feel used, and neither do the people in your network. So, identify ways you can add value to your network, offer them some assistance, or even just show support.

If you're thinking you don't have any value or anything to offer your network, here are some ideas:

- Have they released a book or product? Purchase one and share some feedback.
- Do they have a non-profit or community outreach organization? Volunteer, donate, or simply share the mission with other people you know.
- Do you have a special skill that aligns with their business? Offer your expertise for a period of time.

The goal is to make it easier on the people in your network to help you. Even better, for them to offer their help without even being asked. By you being willing to offer them value, they will be more likely to reciprocate and also vouch for you with their own networks.

7. **Always have your pitch(es) ready.** So far, we've talked about creating organic connections and nurturing relationships, but it's important to deliver the right impression when you first meet these contacts.

When you introduce yourself and share why you're connecting, you should have a thirty-second elevator pitch that directly showcases who you are and the value you bring in an intriguing way. Even if you don't feel you have a lot of experience to offer, you can share your accolades. As an example, if you won awards in sports or the athletic programs you were a part of earned recognition, you can add that to your elevator pitch to show you come from a background of excellence.

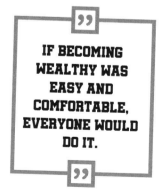

IF BECOMING WEALTHY WAS EASY AND COMFORTABLE, EVERYONE WOULD DO IT.

Pro Tip: Beyond your initial elevator pitch where you introduce yourself and what you bring to the table, you should always have your "ask" elevator pitch ready should the opportunity present itself. One of my favorite sayings is, "When you stay ready, you don't have to get ready." You never know when you may get into a conversation with one of your connections, and they ask directly, "How can I best help you?", "What can I do for you?", or "What do you need?" You would never want to be in the situation where you're fumbling over your words and potentially miss the opportunity.

To build your "ask" elevator pitch, go all the way back to the first strategy where you set your goals. During that exercise, you defined where you want to go and what you want to achieve. Your next step is now to tailor your goals to the particular person's skills, expertise, or influence. For example, let's say your original goal was to secure a new career in the tech industry, and you connected with a hiring manager at Google. Your "ask" elevator pitch when they offer to help would be centered on obtaining a job opportunity at Google in the specific department/team you want to work in, and why you think you would be the right fit.

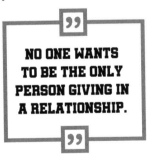

NO ONE WANTS TO BE THE ONLY PERSON GIVING IN A RELATIONSHIP.

After reading through these strategies, it may seem like there are a lot of pieces to networking, but if I had one final piece of advice, it would be for you not to think about networking as something to stress over or fear. Shift your mindset to think of it as building a team—*your* team. Success is not a solo sport. Earning the kind of money you desire is impossible to do if you are working alone.

Think about it this way: you don't win games or championships as an athlete on your own. You have to rely on your teammates and coaches to help get the job done.

Now, in the next chapter of your life, you need a team of people you can tap into and rely on to help you make the best career and business moves possible. The right team will partner with you to ensure those moves will be successful.

"If you want to go fast, go alone.
If you want to go far, go together."
— African Proverb

ABOUT JULIA

Julia C. Rock is a career and leadership development coach who has helped hundreds of ambitious Black and POC professionals break through career plateaus to secure six-figure salaries and fulfilling job opportunities.

She is also a Certified Professional Resume Writer (CPRW) and a Certified Employment Interview Professional (CEIP).

Through her company, Rock Career Development, she now helps Black and POC basketball players at the professional and collegiate level translate their existing skills into high-paying, in-demand careers.

By using her signature coaching methods, clients are able to secure dream positions while earning their worth and then some.

Julia has been featured in several major publications, including Fortune, Business Insider, Monster.com, xoNecole, and Blavity.

CHAPTER ELEVEN

THE GAME IS PLAYED ABOVE THE SHOULDERS

By Austin O. Sanders

I started playing football at nine years old. It was one of the first things where I felt talented. It seemed like everyone I knew, younger and older, thought football was the best thing for me to do.

All I wanted to do in high school was to earn a scholarship to play football at a Division 1 college. I didn't even think about a major. I just wanted to keep playing and say that I was a D1 athlete.

I was on the way back home from a visit to a Division 2 school in North Carolina. I was too talented to be going there. I spoke with the coach before leaving the campus, and he cornered me by asking me whether I was coming to the school or not. He said he needed an answer before I got in the car. I didn't know how to stop people from pushing me into making decisions at that time in my life, so I reluctantly committed to attending his school in the fall.

On the way back home, I felt confused as to why I didn't have any better offers since I was performing well in games against the top-tier talent found throughout Dekalb County schools in Georgia. My train of thought was interrupted by my phone's ringtone. It was the offensive line coach from a school in Mississippi. The last time I spoke to him, I lied and told him I was going on a visit to North Carolina A&T since I was sure he knew who they were.

He asked me how I'd liked the campus. I knew he was gauging if they'd offered me a scholarship, so I just told him it was beautiful. It felt strange lying like this. I didn't see why all these coaches beat around the bush so much. It made more sense for him to just offer me the scholarship or tell me what I needed to do to get it. For some reason, people didn't talk straight to me very often though, especially the colligate coaches.

After some silence, he asked if NCAT had decided to offer me a scholarship. I told him they had. He paused and told me to give him ten minutes to call back. It only took him five.

"We'd like to offer you a full scholarship," he said as soon as I picked up the phone. It was so strange he couldn't have just done that in the first place without all that needless small talk, but I had been told that's just how the game goes. Either way, I finally got my D1 offer. Mission accomplished.

I attended the last semester of summer school because my mom said it would help my transition process. I was so excited to be away from home and embarking on this experience I had heard so much about. The summer workouts weren't quite what I was expecting, but they were difficult, nonetheless. The first workout was hectic, but after that, it wasn't anything too crazy. I just had to make it through the dreaded fall camp.

Within the first few days of camp, I got the opportunity to play against one of the starting defensive ends in a one-on-one pass-protection drill. I had heard in high school that the game speeds up in college, but this was my first time experiencing it. It seemed like the whistle blew, I blinked, and I was picking myself up off the ground.

This was during a time when two-a-days (two practices in one day) were still legal, so I knew I was going to have to see him again very soon. Losing was one thing, but losing to the point of being on the ground was something entirely different, so I needed to make sure it did not happen again. I replayed the drill over and over in my mind, looking for all the possible mistakes I could improve on. He moved so fast when the play started, I forgot to read the body language to see what move he was going to use. I had lost my cool and panicked, which is not particularly good for thinking ahead.

Before the next practice, I took a mental inventory of the things I needed to worry about. My opponent was not exceptionally large for a defensive linemen so I ruled out the need to worry about him running straight through me if my center of gravity was low and balanced. That meant he was more than likely going to use speed moves. With that analysis, I won the next time I went against him. Then I won again the next practice. And then it became a pattern.

Though I was doing well on the field, I was not enjoying my campus experience in the

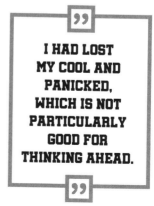

I HAD LOST MY COOL AND PANICKED, WHICH IS NOT PARTICULARLY GOOD FOR THINKING AHEAD.

slightest. I'd need another book with more room than just one chapter to go into detail, but after I lost thirty pounds that I had no intention of losing, and I really paid attention to the events going on around me, I knew that school was not the place for me.

I began searching for opportunities elsewhere. I authored an email that explained my situation and attached my highlights from that season. The subject line read: Offensive Lineman, 6'4", 300 pounds, 3.0 GPA, Seeking Transfer. I'd heard somewhere that email subject lines determined if people opened the email, so I thought that would be dazzling enough for coaches looking for good linemen. Who cared if I was shorter than 6'4" and actually weighed 270 pounds?

After sending more than 250 emails and having numerous discussions with coaches all over the nation, I negotiated a full athletic scholarship to Mercer University. This felt like my biggest accomplishment yet. I honestly felt like a superstar in my head.

THIS FELT LIKE MY BIGGEST ACCOMPLISHMENT YET.

After my experience in Mississippi, my wants were much simpler than they were in high school, and Mercer provided me with virtually everything I was looking for in a school. I remember shedding a tear after being told we had smoothies waiting on us in the locker room at the end of practice.

With so much less to worry about, I was able to put all my energy into perfecting my craft. This resulted in me receiving All-Conference honor awards for three years in a row. I could tell my name was starting to buzz in certain rooms.

By my senior year, I spoke to scouts from the Baltimore Ravens, Cincinnati Bengals, New York Giants, and Tampa Bay Buccaneers. After they saw me walking and talking to someone with one of those

"32" logos on their shirts, younger players looked at me with eyes of admiration. It was all very flattering to the athlete in me, but to me as an individual, it felt more like something other people enjoyed witnessing. Each time I spoke to an NFL scout, I viewed it as a surprise interview for an extreme job that paid me a lot because I was risking the one body I get in life every day I come to work. I felt ashamed to not feel as happy as everyone said they were for me, so I tried not to speak about it too much.

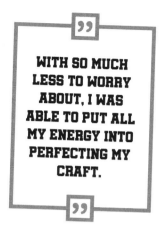

> WITH SO MUCH LESS TO WORRY ABOUT, I WAS ABLE TO PUT ALL MY ENERGY INTO PERFECTING MY CRAFT.

I didn't feel that many people had really experienced that kind of juice and how pointless it all was. And, as Big KRIT has said, "What was the point of trying to explain the summertime to someone that has only seen snow," right?

Honestly, my junior year is when my feelingof enjoyment began to dwindle. I knew I was done when I injured my knee with four weeks left in my senior season. With so little time left, I was doing my best to push through with the little patience I still had.

I had been taking 800-milligram ibuprofen tablets before every padded practice and before every game since I first sprained my ankle around the third game of an eleven-game season to help me tolerate the pain of playing on it. I had to get my ankle wrapped three different times just to provide the stability my joint now lacked, but I still tried to *think* optimistically. I'd tell myself things like. *"All I have to do is make it through these last four games carefully and then I could have a shot at getting to the Justice League (NFL)."*

But then I got hurt again at practice. This time, it was my knee on the opposite leg. Someone fell into it from the side during an exercise called "Inside Drill". Luckily, I was wearing some joint-stabilizing knee braces, so none of my ligaments were torn. Instead, I left the field with a bone bruise in my knee. Even with such a lucky break, I remember limping to my car the next day and barely being able bend my leg enough to drive. It was similar to the time I sprained my MCL a year or so prior.

I sat in my room with my knee in a thick brace *thinking* about still going to the NFL. *If my knee is feeling like this now, what is playing against even stronger people at the highest level going to feel like?* That's when I knew I was done with football.

I bring my background up because understanding history gives context to the present. I understand the feelings that can come with leaving the comfort zone you have known for most of your life. I know what it is like to attach your identity to something so temporary.

People saying things like, "College is the best time of your life", was so confusing to me. It was a cool experience. I enjoyed many of the amenities provided to me and all the free time I had while I was in school. But it made me feel that the remainder of my years would be worse. The way I understood the saying,it meant that if I lived to be seventy-eight, I would never be as happy over the next fifty-eight years as I was from ages eighteen to twenty-two! I didn't want to wrap my mind around that, and I still don't.

The only thing I could really think about in my new retirement was that now I didn't know how to make money. I knew that people went and got a job or created a job for themselves, but I didn't know *how*.

I had spent fourteen years becoming an expert on offensive line play in football. I was really good at stopping speed rushes, spin moves, pushing people against their will, etc. I knew how safety movement predicted what the defensive ends were going to do. I was good at foreseeing if I was going to get a spin move, bullrush, push-pull, or speed move within someone's first three steps. But these skills didn't seem very transferable.

I felt like I was starting over from zero. I wondered: *did I just waste my time running into other people all these years?* All that I have now are creaky joints that hurt when it rained, poor short-term memory, and above-average knowledge regarding football and weightlifting. Or so I thought.

After wallowing in my despair for a couple of weeks and blaming others for my lack of knowledge, I decided that these thoughts were not changing my situation, and were not very helpful. I've never been a fan of doing things I could not see the point of, and wallowing was not moving me in any direction I liked, so it had no point.

Being curious enough to become an expert in football yielded pretty good results for me. It gave me a chance to extend my childhood and to hold off responsibilities and bills for five years after high school while I meandered and learned useful skills. It gave me a chance to mature as an individual before I had to really step out into the world of consequences. Being curious provided me with opportunity and time, both of which are invaluable.

The curiosity and desire to learn about a specific thing like football opened many doors for me. If I took this same energy and intention and applied it to anything else, why wouldn't I get similar results?

With this understanding, I felt hopeful. What I needed to do now was understand my current situation. We can't know where we're headed without knowing where we want to go, right? Since I was taking a trip into the unknown, I had to pack my bag with things I did know, or at least what I thought I knew. And as I made this list in my head, it brought up more unknowns.

I needed money, but how do people actually make money? I knew that someone could get a job for it, or they could create a job themselves, but *how?*

My credit score was in the low 500s because of past mistakes, but *how* do I actually go about improving that score and paying down my debts?

Living in my own space in school was so liberating, but I did not have to pay anything monetarily. My sweat equity and physical sacrifice paid the bill. How then could I afford a comfortable home so I could live by my rules and standards?

I have a graduate degree in media studies and a graduate degree in organizational leadership, but *how* do I make money with them? How much can I make with them? Am I even capable of doing the jobs that align with these degrees?

These were some of the questions I asked myself. I did not know how to get the answers, but I knew that once I got the answers to these questions, I would be in a much better position. I had one more semester (five months) to enjoy the apartment I did not pay for and the cafeteria I had unlimited access to. Now was the time to make some mistakes and figure out what I did *not* want to do.

Being the wonderful person she is, my older cousin, Bethany, pulled some strings to get my resume created by a professional resume writer. At the same time, my mom got one of her friend's sons, John, to help me create my résumé. I had no idea how to structure it for a specific position, but luckily, he was much more experienced in corporate climbing than I, so he gave me a heap of information about it. A good amount of the information went over my head, but I knew enough to know it would help me one day.

With their help, I had a resume that looked like I might know how to do a little something. I took that resume and sent it to every job opening that caught my eye on Indeed.com.

> **NOW WAS THE TIME TO MAKE SOME MISTAKES AND FIGURE OUT WHAT I DID NOT WANT TO DO.**

One day, while doing this random spray n' pray style of applying, I gave one of my friends a ride home from work. For the sake of this story, we'll call her "Bliss". When Bliss got in the car, she asked if I could drop her off at another place before I took her home. I replied, "Sure."

She directed me to a large building about five minutes away and said she'd be right back. She came out fifteen minutes later with a grin on her face. I asked, "What did you just do in there?" Bliss replied, "I just got an interview!"

I tilted my head and furrowed my brows. I had to know more. "What does that mean? Please explain this to me," I said as I leaned in with anticipation. She told me she applied for a job on Indeed and went to speak to someone in person about the position. The building I took her to was the address that was listed when she researched the business.

She approached the first person she saw with her resume in hand, introduced herself, and asked about the opening for a front office coordinator.

The woman responded, "How did you know about that position? We haven't released it to the public."

Bliss told her about the opening she saw online, and they came to understand that someone created a false job and used another company's business address as their own.

By the end of their conversation, the woman said they planned to go to a temp-agency to hire the front office coordinator, but since she enjoyed Bliss' personality so much, she wanted to set up an interview.

I was quiet for a moment because my mind was connecting the dots. If Bliss had only put in an application online without coming in person, she would have missed this opportunity. Her personality is what opened the door for her.

Bliss talked her way into a position that paid $17/hr., which was a lot better than the job she was currently doing for $10/hr. She also found out that the last person who worked in the position got a promotion to project manager after a year with an annual salary of $55,000. All that was now possible for her because she went in-person and spoke up.

With this information, I started writing down the address of each job I applied for so I could go in-person and do what I called the "Bliss Method"–physically showing up and throwing around some personality.

To prepare for my in-person appearances, I went and bought some collared shirts and slacks from Walmart. I visited every job I applied for online. I spoke to the first employee I made eye contact with. I introduced myself and asked them if they knew who I could speak with about whatever job opening it was that I had applied for earlier. Many people took me to the exact person responsible for filling these positions.

Before too long, I was getting invited back for interviews regularly. When speaking to these people, they would mention there had been hundreds of people applying to every job opening online, and how rare it was that someone came in-person. It almost felt like I was skipping the line.

In about four months, I started and quit about four positions. I worked as a management trainee at Waffle House, a car salesman, a front desk attendant at a hotel, and a couple of other roles. I learned about the program at Waffle House and the front desk position at the hotel from a job fair at Mercer.

At the job fair, I made sure to speak with someone at every table. I'd ask them about the job opening, as well as how they got to their current position in the company (since I knew stories contain loads of information, and people typically like talking about themselves). The owner of the hotel later told me he heard about how I was working the room and that was the exact reason he wanted to hire me. I also left a resume at the hotel, gave a copy to them at the job fair, and applied online, which helped to show my thoroughness. It seemed like the Bliss Method was working.

I stopped working at Waffle House because touching plates with leftover food grossed me out. I stopped working at the dealership because I don't care to talk about cars, and I left the hotel because I didn't ask for enough money. I didn't know how much I would need to live comfortably.

At this time, I just moved in with my homie, Sherman, so I knew my money was going to need to count since I was about to be responsible for bills. The place where we lived in Macon was extremely affordable for two men still new to their professional careers, but once I saw the bills and did some math, I knew I had asked for too little money. I only asked for $13/hr., but looking back on it, I should have requested $25/hr. just to see how they would have responded.

I was not thinking about it at the time, but the owner and the manager really liked me, so they would have counter-offered in the worst-case scenario. Half of my interview consisted of the owner telling me how he learned to make money and seize opportunities because of how close-knit his family and community were.

I got so much information from him because I asked him, "How did you get to where you are now?" when he asked me if I had any questions for him. I could tell he liked my curiosity, but I did not understand the leverage that this gave me in salary negotiations. I could have even asked for more. The worst they could have said was "no".

I ended up leaving after a couple of months to work at a shopping center for $15/hr. in asset protection. The owner of the hotel told me how he helped an employee from my school get a job as an orchestra director at Disney after two years of working for him since he was an outstanding employee. I made a mistake leaving so hastily since there was a tremendous upside to the job, but I did not understand these things at the time. All I knew was I wanted more money after being responsible for half of a water bill and electric bill for the first time.

The bulk of the position in asset protection was stopping people from stealing things from the store. I quickly learned I did not have the heart or desire for this line of work during my training. We caught someone stealing watches on camera. After we escorted him to a room and retrieved the items, he told us he was stealing to make enough money to take care of his kid-sister. The guy looked to be about seventeen or eighteen years old, with stress on his mind.

He explained how there was a gang war happening where he lived in Macon, and his mother was out of the picture since she had fallen victim to addiction. He said he was just doing what he could to survive all of this.

If it were up to me, I would have let him go free, but the people that were training us called the police to identify him since the guy did not have any ID. When the police ran his fingerprints, they discovered he was in his 30s from Florida with a warrant for child molestation. Before they took him away, he took a long look at each of us. The stare seemed equally enraged and thoughtful.

My homie, Deezy, told me he was remembering each of our faces later that day when I regaled the tale to him. At that point, I knew I was not going to stay at that job much longer. Fifteen bucks per hour was not enough for me to be worrying about vendettas.

Luckily, I had been contacted about a position as an operations manager at a property management company—whatever that meant. It was a position I randomly applied for without reading the job description, which is not wise. "Operations manager" sounded like a good title to me, so I applied without giving it a second thought.

When the owner, Ben, called me for a phone interview, I went ahead and addressed my lack of experience. I explained how honing my discipline, problem-solving skills, and ability to learn in football would make me a great candidate for any team. He responded by assuring me my lack of experience wouldn't be a problem since he, himself, had no experience in the field before starting the company only six years prior.

During the interview with him and his partner, Jake, they asked me why I was a good fit for the position. Just as I did at the hotel, I told the two of them I was seeking to become an expert at something, and this curiosity was going to help me be great in whatever position I was in. I got a call the next week informing me I got the position.

I was getting answers to the questions I listed earlier. I saw that I could get any kind of job if I could simply convince them I was worth teaching. My rent was extremely cheap, especially since having a roommate allowed me to only pay a portion instead of the whole bill. Splitting those bills allowed me to save enough money to start putting some of it toward assets, like this very book that you are reading.

Sherman and I ended up moving after we learned the hard way that one must pay a little more for a quality environment. Still, given the circumstances, we were doing very well two young brothas figuring things out.

My good friend from high school, Johnny, started schooling me on how credit worked and put together a plan to raise my score. I didn't realize it, but I had been scared to use credit cards because I only heard about how it could ruin people financially and not about how it could be a tool when used correctly.

He also told me to figure out what the previous person in my role did well and did poorly. If I could improve on what they did in the first three months of working there, it would make me look like a great investment.

I didn't even have to ask about the things the previous guy did because my coworkers seemed very willing to tell me about it. I would just listen. I understood the things he liked about the job, the things he did not like about the job, his strengths, and his weaknesses within the first few weeks by simply listening when someone started talking about it. It's almost like they heard my friend's advice as well and wanted to make the process easier for me.

I was nervous about messing up, since I had no idea what I was doing. Then, I actually did start messing up. I broke a window screen trying to install a portable air conditioner. I lost a couple sets of keys (they were about $150 to replace) in the same month. I was costing the company money, and I was not sure if I was going to be fired soon.

Instead of getting the boot, I was given pointers to do better the next time I ran into similar situations. When I spoke to people with more work experience, they told me about how everyone makes mistakes when doing something for the first time because that was a part of the learning process.

It took me back to the first game I played as a starter in high school. It was a scrimmage against North Gwinnett High School, and I was going against an All-American defensive end. For the entire first quarter, that man gave me the *bidness*, and there was nothing I could do about it. I was so flustered I couldn't remember the plays. I was so caught up, I couldn't think until I went to the bench and my offensive coordinator, Coach Reggie Ball, looked me in my eyes and asked, "You ready to start playing now?"

I didn't do much better for the rest of the game, but that sentence reengaged my brain so I could start learning from my mistakes.

In a similar manner, I opened my mind to the information I was receiving and worked to forgive myself for mistakes I was bound to make while learning. I told my father about it, and he suggested I start journaling these thoughts because, "you never know who might want to hear about the story."

It has been two years since I started that job. Since then, I've learned a bit more about myself, my profession, and my learning process. I've learned to invest a bit more and how to speak more effectively. There are a few books that have helped me gain a better direction and understanding of my journey.

Reading *The Four Agreements: A Practical Guide to Personal Freedom* by Don Miguel Ruiz has helped me forgive myself and others.

I WAS SO FLUSTERED I COULDN'T REMEMBER THE PLAYS.

The Big Leap: Conquer Your Hidden Fear and Take Life to the Next Level by Gay Hendricks helped me to start identifying the things that made me afraid of succeeding in everything I attempted.

I did not realize it before, but when I thought of being extremely successful, I automatically thought of cliches like "More money, more problems" or "It's lonely at the top". This book allowed me to understand how to define the causes of these self-sabotaging thoughts.

Never Split The Difference: Negotiating As If Your Life Depended On It by Chris Voss explained the power of silence to me. It helped me to understand that everything is negotiable if you know the right combination of words.

The information in this book has actually helped me make $3,000 extra in a business deal. I might speak more about that in my next book.

I hope my story assists you on your journey. Remember:

Always be open to new information because we can never know too much. If you can get help, never be afraid to do so. Everyone and everything that has ever been on this planet is a resource to you.

Like my father told me, "If you have something to say, say it. If you don't, then don't say anything."

ABOUT AUSTIN

Austin O. Sanders is a three-time, all-conference offensive tackle footballer who played at Mercer University. During his athletic career, he developed skills that helped him navigate the football playing field. When it came time to transition from sports to the sport of life, the same skills that allowed Austin to excel in his sport have continued to be useful.

While working to best utilize the talents that became visible to him during his playing years, he learned he could use his experiences and skills to make a difference in others' lives. By combining his want to help others and his storytelling ability, the chapter entitled, "The Game is Played Above The Shoulders" was manifested. It is Austin's hope that his experiences can help other athletes reclaim their identity and adapt with life.

CONCLUSION

In order to create your future, it's imperative you not only study your own past, but also study the past of those who have come before you.

John C. Maxwell says, "A wise person learns from his mistakes. A wiser one learns from others' mistakes. But the wisest person of all learns from others's successes."

The truth is, there is no one-size-fits-all approach to life for anyone. "Success" is a broad term that each of us defines differently. This book is a must-read for athletes at any stage in their careers.

By compiling all these lessons into one book, I sincerely hope you're able to take bits and pieces from each section that you can carry with you for the rest of your life.

All the contributing authors used real-life examples, methods, and tools we've used during and after our days competing in the athletic arena.

These chapters discuss ways to implement your skills and offer concrete advice the authors have used to get them to the next level. Anyone can apply these skills immediately.

Whether you are a current or former athlete, if you apply the lessons from this book, I have no doubt you'll be well on your way to earning six figures, and much more.

We want to encourage you to share this book with someone who needs it. Share it with a friend, a family member, a former teammate, a coach, or anyone who works directly with athletes.

Each of us is always looking for better opportunities to serve the athletic community, and this book is just one of the many ways we aim to do so.

Any size university or professional organization could use the lessons in this book for the betterment of their athletes, helping them to develop into well-rounded individuals.

If you or anyone you know is working through their transition into life after sports, please don't hesitate to reach out to any of these authors. We are here for you!

Not only do we want to make an impact, but we also want to make a difference in the lives of current and former athletes by helping them get the results they deserve.

Made in the USA
Columbia, SC
23 November 2022

71961458R00091